CONTENTS

The Indian Ocean 1942

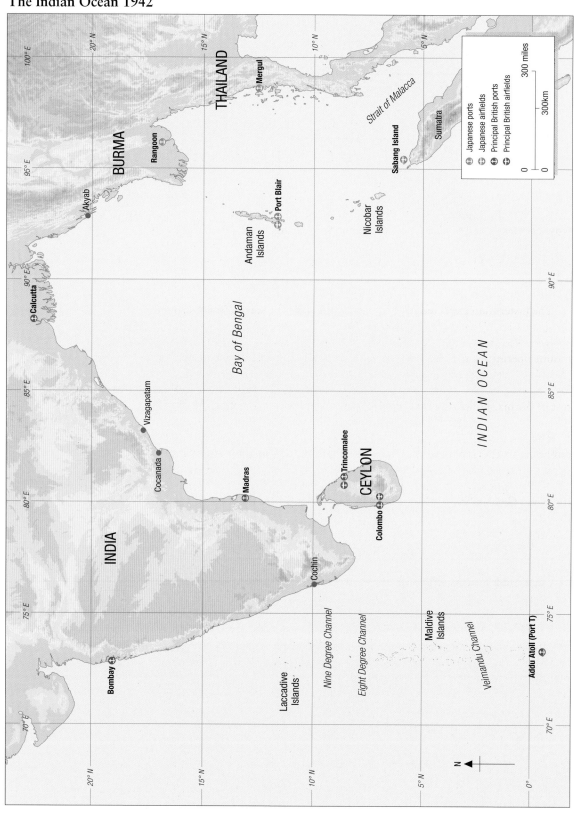

100° E · 95° E · 90° E · 85° E · 80° E · 75° E · 70° E

20° N · 15° N · 10° N · 5° N · 0°

THAILAND

BURMA

Mergui

Rangoon

Akyab

Strait of Malacca

Sumatra

Sabang Island

Nicobar Islands

Port Blair

Andaman Islands

Calcutta

Bay of Bengal

INDIAN OCEAN

Vizagapatam

Cocanada

Madras

Trincomalee

CEYLON

Colombo

INDIA

Cochin

Bombay

Laccadive Islands

Nine Degree Channel

Eight Degree Channel

Maldive Islands

Veimandu Channel

Addu Atoll (Port T)

N

Japanese ports	
Japanese airfields	
Principal British ports	
Principal British airfields	

300 miles

300km

0 · 0

CAMPAIGN 396

JAPAN'S INDIAN OCEAN RAID 1942

The Allies' Lowest Ebb

MARK STILLE

ILLUSTRATED BY JIM LAURIER
Series editor Nikolai Bogdanovic

OSPREY PUBLISHING
Bloomsbury Publishing Plc
Kemp House, Chawley Park, Cumnor Hill, Oxford OX2 9PH, UK
29 Earlsfort Terrace, Dublin 2, Ireland
1385 Broadway, 5th Floor, New York, NY 10018, USA
E-mail: info@ospreypublishing.com
www.ospreypublishing.com

OSPREY is a trademark of Osprey Publishing Ltd

First published in Great Britain in 2023

A catalogue record for this book is available from the British Library.

ISBN: PB 9781472854186; eBook 9781472854179; ePDF 9781472854193;
XML 9781472854209

23 24 25 26 27   10 9 8 7 6 5 4 3 2 1

Maps by Bounford.com
3D BEVs by Paul Kime
Index by Angela Hall
Typeset by PDQ Digital Media Solutions, Bungay, UK
Printed and bound in India by Replika Press Private Ltd.

Osprey Publishing supports the Woodland Trust, the UK's leading woodland
conservation charity.

To find out more about our authors and books visit
www.ospreypublishing.com. Here you will find extracts, author
interviews, details of forthcoming events and the option to sign up for
our newsletter.

Artist's note

Readers can find out more about the work of illustrator Jim Laurier via the
following website:
www.jimlaurier.com

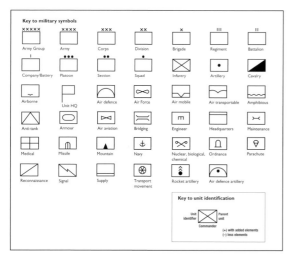

FRONT COVER ILLUSTRATION: Val dive-bombers from carrier
Shokaku led by Lieutenant-Commander Takahashi attack HMS
Hermes. (Jim Laurier)
TITLE PAGE: The destruction of British heavy cruisers *Cornwall* and
Dorsetshire was the height of Operation *C* for the Striking Force.
This Japanese photo shows the cruisers under attack and burning.
(Imperial Japanese Navy, now in the Public Domain)

ORIGINS OF THE CAMPAIGN

Even before the Japanese had completed their conquest of British Malaya and Singapore and the Dutch East Indies, plans were being made for the invasion of Burma. Expansion into Burma was viewed as vital to provide a strategic buffer for the just-conquered southern resource areas and as a means to cut off supply routes into China. The problem for the Japanese was that adequate forces were not immediately available for an invasion of Burma.

The faster than expected pace of operations since the start of the war made the Japanese hasten plans to invade Burma. The result was an agreement between the Imperial Army (IJA) and Navy (IJN) on 22 January 1942 to mount operations to seize key points in Burma. After seizing the airfields in southern Burma and the key port of Rangoon, the IJN agreed to move two divisions by sea to Rangoon to allow the IJA to prosecute operations into the rest of Burma. Following that, the IJN was tasked with protecting the Army's sea lines of communications (SLOC) into Burma.

Though it was not part of Japanese pre-war planning, it quickly became apparent to the Japanese that the Andaman Islands in the eastern Indian Ocean were critical to the defence of the southern resource areas and the SLOCs supporting Japanese troops in Burma. Accordingly, on 4 February the Navy General Staff informed the Combined Fleet that it planned to seize the islands. Three days later, orders were issued to that effect.

Another emergent addition to Japanese plans in the initial stage of the war was the seizure of Christmas Island, a volcanic island located 220nm south of Java in the Indian Ocean. Its location placed it astride the SLOC between India and Australia. It also could provide depth for the defence of the southern resource area. On 14 March, the Navy General Staff issued orders to the Combined Fleet to capture the island.

There were other IJN planners that advocated far larger operations in the Indian Ocean. Strategic planning in the IJN was complicated by the fact that it was not done by a single entity. Formal responsibility for strategic planning rested with the First Section of the Navy General Staff. In reality, the commander of the Combined Fleet, Admiral Yamamoto Isoroku, had a more significant role. Members of the Navy General Staff advocated for a significant expansion of operations in the Indian Ocean, including taking Ceylon. Such an undertaking promised massive potential benefits. British SLOCs in the Indian Ocean would be cut and the British position in the Persian Gulf threatened.

A major advance to the west was not part of Japan's pre-war expansion plans. The IJA failed to support it. Most importantly, Yamamoto had

Kirishima and *Akagi* pictured in April 1939. The speed of the Kongo-class battleships made them ideal for carrier task force operations and the Striking Force always had at least two of those ships assigned to it. (Yamato Museum)

different ideas for Phase Two of the war. He was convinced that the greatest threat to Japan and its new acquisitions was the United States Navy (USN) in the form of the Pacific Fleet. Yamamoto therefore advocated for a major push in the Central Pacific with the principal aim of drawing the Pacific Fleet into a decisive battle.

Though Yamamoto was focused on his Central Pacific offensive, he saw the benefit of supporting actions in other areas. One of these was a pre-emptive strike against the British Eastern Fleet in Ceylon. During planning for operations in Burma and against the Andaman Islands, the need to neutralize any British naval threat in the region came into focus. The opportunity to conduct a major raid against the British in the Indian Ocean readily presented itself since the Combined Fleet's most powerful force, the carriers of the First Air Fleet, were already in the region supporting the final phases of the operation to seize the Dutch East Indies. By the first week of March, the Combined Fleet gave its blessing for a major raid into the Indian Ocean. The First Air Fleet was tasked to destroy the British Eastern Fleet in harbour at Ceylon in a surprise attack. Concurrently, surface warships would ravage British shipping in the Bay of Bengal. The IJN's Indian Ocean adventure was designated Operation C.

The British were fully aware of the importance of holding Ceylon and were convinced that its loss would jeopardize their position in the Indian Ocean and the Persian Gulf. Since February they had made frantic efforts to strengthen both the Eastern Fleet and the defences on the island. The British recognized the possibility of an invasion of Ceylon but assessed a Japanese raid into the region as more likely. In mid-March, British intelligence discerned Japanese plans for just such a raid. Both sides now prepared for a major clash in the area off Ceylon.

CHRONOLOGY

1942

9 March Admiral Yamamoto issues orders for the Indian Ocean operation.

19 March Operation *U*, the movement of two divisions by sea to Rangoon, commences.

23 March The Japanese invasion of the Andaman Islands meets no resistance.

26 March The Striking Force departs Staring Bay in the Dutch East Indies.

30 March The Eastern Fleet departs Port T to counter the expected 1 April Japanese raid on Ceylon.

31 March The Japanese occupy Christmas Island.

1 April Malaya Unit Striking Force departs Mergui in southern Burma.

2 April Somerville abandons his planned ambush of the Japanese and heads back to Port T.

4 April 1200hrs – Force A arrives at Port T.
1500hrs – Force B arrives at Port T.
1555hrs – Catalina spots the Striking Force south-east of Ceylon.

5 April 0000hrs – Force A departs Port T and heads for the reported location of the Japanese fleet.
0700hrs – Force B departs Port T.
0740–0820hrs – Japanese strike of 38 dive-bombers, 53 level bombers and 36 Zeros attack Colombo.
1000hrs – Japanese floatplane spots 'two cruiser-like vessels' west of the Striking Force.
1338–1358hrs – 53 dive-bombers sink *Cornwall* and *Dorsetshire* south-west of Colombo.
1340–1442hrs – *Ryujo* aircraft sink one and damage two merchants in the Bay of Bengal.
1400hrs – Four Albacores dispatched from Force A to search for the Striking Force.
1600hrs – Albacores detect the Striking Force.
1726hrs – Somerville turns the Eastern Fleet away from the Japanese; at this point the two fleets were only 100nm apart.
1930hrs – Additional Albacore launched but it fails to gain contact with the Striking Force.

6 April Beginning at 0600hrs – Ships and aircraft from the Malaya Unit Striking Force destroy 20 merchants in the Bay of Bengal 1300hrs – Somerville detaches ships to rescue the crews of *Cornwall* and *Dorsetshire*.

8 April 1100hrs – Eastern Fleet arrives in Port T.
1520hrs – Catalina spots Striking Force 475nm south-east of Trincomalee.
1755hrs – Arbuthnot orders 12 ships in Trincomalee to depart.

9 April 0100hrs – *Hermes* and *Vampire* depart Trincomalee.
0200hrs – Force B departs Port T for safety in East Africa.
0600hrs – Force A departs Port T for safety in Bombay.
0708hrs – Catalina spots the Striking Force 200nm east of Trincomalee.
0715–0820hrs – 91 level bombers and 41 Zeros attack Trincomalee.
0755hrs – Japanese floatplane spots *Hermes* and *Vampire*.
0820hrs – 11 Blenheims depart the Racecourse to attack the Striking Force.
0843–0853hrs – 85 dive-bombers and 9 Zeros take off to attack *Hermes*.
1040hrs – Attack on *Hermes* begins.
1045hrs – Nine Blenheims surprise and attack the Striking Force with no success.
1055hrs – *Hermes* sinks; attack on *Vampire* begins.
1100hrs – Tanker *British Sergeant* attacked by dive-bombers.
1102hrs – *Vampire* breaks in two.
1205hrs – *Soryu* dive-bombers attack *Athelstane* and *Norviken*.
1208hrs – *Soryu* dive-bombers attack *Hollyhock*.
1215hrs – *Norviken*'s crew abandons ship.
1215–1250hrs – British fighters engage *Soryu*'s dive-bombers and destroy four.
1217hrs – *Hollyhock* sinks.
1300hrs – *British Sergeant* sinks.
1430hrs – *Athelstane* sinks.

11 April Malaya Unit arrives in Singapore.

13 April Striking Force departs the Indian Ocean.

OPPOSING COMMANDERS

JAPANESE

Admiral Yamamoto Isoroku had been the commander of the Combined Fleet since 1939. His standing was high in April 1942 following the stunning attack on Pearl Harbor and the conquest of all of Japan's First Operational Phase objectives. He was not a supporter of any major Indian Ocean commitment since his eyes were firmly set on the Second Operational Phase objectives in the Central and South Pacific and the all-important destruction of the USN's Pacific Fleet.

As the commander of the Second Fleet, **Vice Admiral Kondo Nobutake** was one of Yamamoto's principal commanders. He was allocated the bulk of the Combined Fleet (becoming the Southern Expeditionary Force) and was placed in charge of covering the invasions of Malaya and the Dutch East Indies. Despite some minor glitches, this was accomplished ahead of schedule and at a very low cost. When the IJN decided to mount an Indian Ocean foray, Kondo was placed in charge of the operation. He was by all accounts a capable officer and shared the aggressive outlook held by almost all senior IJN officers.

Kondo's force had two principal components. Commander of the Malaya Unit was **Vice Admiral Ozawa Jisaburo**. He possessed the operational and tactical skills required to accomplish the missions of his force. Ozawa was a pre-war air power advocate who later went on to command the Combined Fleet's carrier force from November 1942 until November 1944. He was undoubtedly one of the finest IJN officers of the war. One of Ozawa's principal commanders was Rear Admiral Kurita Takeo, commander of the 7th Cruiser Division. His performance was uneven during the Dutch East Indies campaign. Later in the war, he led the Combined Fleet's last major effort at the battle of Leyte Gulf.

Admiral Yamamoto Isoroku, commander of the Combined Fleet, opposed any large-scale offensive into the Indian Ocean. However, he gave his blessing to using a significant portion of the Combined Fleet for a major raid into the region with the goal of destroying the Royal Navy's Eastern Fleet. (Naval History and History Command)

As the most important component of the Combined Fleet and as the principal force during the Indian Ocean raid, the commander of the Striking Force (or *Kido Butai*) was the most important Japanese command figure of the battle. This post was held by **Vice Admiral Nagumo Chuichi**. He was a sea-going admiral and an expert in torpedo tactics. In April 1941, when the First Air Fleet (the parent command of the Striking Force) was formed, Nagumo was appointed as its first commander. He received this job not because he had any expertise or even any experience in carrier or any type of aviation operations, but because he was the senior unassigned vice admiral at the time. In fact, many of the IJN's aviation command billets were held by non-aviators. What set Nagumo aside was his cautious nature. Some of his subordinates also remarked on his indecisiveness. Given his lack of aviation experience and his indecisiveness, he was extremely reliant on his staff. This was unremarkable in the IJN where decisions tended to be made by consensus. Nagumo's chief of staff was **Rear Admiral Kusaka Ryunosuke**. He was also cautious. Though involved in naval aviation since 1926, he was not an aviator and did not possess a deep knowledge of air warfare. The most important figure on Nagumo's staff was the Air Operations Officer, **Commander Genda Minoru**. He was a true aviator who had made his reputation as a fighter pilot and then became one of the driving forces behind the creation of the First Air Fleet. He had the reputation of a tactical genius and an accomplished planner, and was entrusted by Yamamoto with the detailed planning of the Pearl Harbor attack. He also enjoyed the complete trust of Nagumo and was given total freedom in planning operations. Another key individual in Striking Force operations was **Commander Fuchida Mitsuo**. As the senior aviator he was given command of major strikes and his on-scene recommendations were critical to the success or failure of these strikes.

ABOVE LEFT
Vice Admiral Kondo Nobutake was commander of the Southern Expeditionary Force during the opening phase of the war. He provided the forces used for the Indian Ocean raid but did not exercise operational command of those forces. (Naval History and History Command)

ABOVE RIGHT
Vice Admiral Ozawa Jisaburo commanded the Malaya Unit Striking Force with the mission of disrupting British shipping in the Bay of Bengal. Against no resistance, he accomplished this mission, at least temporarily. (Naval History and History Command)

The Striking Force was comprised of three carrier divisions. The First Carrier Division was commanded by Nagumo. The Second Carrier Division was commanded by **Rear Admiral Yamaguchi Tamon**. He was everything Nagumo was not – aggressive and a born leader who was even viewed as a possible successor to Yamamoto. The last and newest carrier division, the Fifth, was entrusted to **Rear Admiral Hara Chuichi**. He was a surface warfare officer who was given command of the Fifth Carrier Division in September 1941. He was known for his fiery temperament and earned the nickname 'King Kong'.

BRITISH

Vice Admiral Sir Geoffrey Layton succeeded Admiral Sir Tom Phillips as Commander-in-Chief Eastern Fleet after Phillips was killed on *Prince of Wales* on 10 December 1941. In early 1942, he became Commander-in-Chief Ceylon. In the words of an official British history, it was 'one of the best appointments Churchill ever made'. He was given full powers to coordinate all aspects of the defence of the island and had authority over all military and civil figures, including the governor of the island. By April 1942, he had made great strides in improving the state of defences on Ceylon.

Vice Admiral Sir James Somerville assumed command of the Eastern Fleet in March 1942 and remained in this position until August 1944. Post-war assessments of British admirals generally hold Somerville as one of the Royal Navy's (RN) top admirals, usually only surpassed by Admiral Sir Andrew Cunningham.

Somerville had wide experience earlier in the war, principally as the commander of Force H operating out of Gibraltar. Force H played a role in

hunting down *Bismarck* in May 1941 and was given the unpalatable mission of attacking the French Fleet in Mers-el-Kebir in July 1940. Force H also conducted many operations inside the Mediterranean. It was one of the first examples of a carrier task group as it always had at least one carrier and a heavy surface ship (fast battleship or a battlecruiser) and other escorts. Somerville was therefore very well acquainted with carrier tactics and with emerging modern technologies like radar. He was viewed by his peers as an inspirational leader, a fine seaman and a good tactician. He was probably the best man available for the job of directing RN operations in the Indian Ocean.

Somerville was fully aware of the perilous situation he was stepping into. On 30 March 1942, he reached his flagship, *Warspite*, off Ceylon. His first message was 'so this is the Eastern Fleet. Never mind. There's many a good tune played on an old fiddle.' This shows Somerville was distinctly aware of the composition of his fleet. During the next week, Somerville exposed the Eastern Fleet, described by his operations officer as a 'rabble', to a high degree of risk. Somerville was given a quality staff with which to conduct his operations. His deputy was **Vice Admiral Sir Algernon Willis**; his chief of staff was **Commodore Ralph Edwards**; the Staff Officer Plans (operations officer) was **Commander Kaye Edden**. All were highly regarded.

The Commander-in-Chief East Indies was **Vice Admiral Geoffrey Arbuthnot**. As an area commander, he was responsible for all naval units not assigned to the Eastern Fleet, all naval bases and the movement of all merchant ships. The principal Royal Air Force (RAF) commander on Ceylon was **Air Vice Marshall John D'Albiac**. In his capacity as Air Officer Commanding 222 Group, he directed the operations of all RAF units and bases on Ceylon and had operational control of the two RN fighter squadrons in the Colombo area. He was co-located with Arbuthnot in a joint operations centre in Colombo.

ABOVE LEFT
Vice Admiral Sir James Somerville, shown here in April 1944 boarding USN carrier *Saratoga*, was commander of the Eastern Fleet from March 1942 until August 1944. In the first two weeks of his tenure, his rashness almost led his command to disaster. (Naval History and History Command)

ABOVE RIGHT
Vice Admiral Geoffrey Arbuthnot was the Commander-in-Chief East Indies during the raid, responsible for all naval forces not assigned to Somerville's Eastern Fleet. Like Somerville, he failed to understand the power of the Japanese forces involved in the raid and his lack of judgement led to avoidable losses. (Public Domain)

OPPOSING FORCES

JAPANESE

The Striking Force

The centrepiece of Combined Fleet operations in the Indian Ocean was the Striking Force under Vice Admiral Nagumo. Since the start of the war it had been active almost non-stop, first attacking Pearl Harbor and then Rabaul in the South Pacific in January 1942. On 8 February, the Striking Force was assigned to the Southern Task Force to support operations in the Dutch East Indies. In this capacity, it conducted massive air strikes against Darwin in northern Australia on 19 February, followed by Tjilatjap on Java on 5 March. Throughout these operations, the Striking Force had not even been spotted by Allied forces, much less attacked. The ability of the Striking Force to mass air power on a single target and the quality of its aircraft and aircrew made it the most powerful naval force on the planet at the time. As powerful as the Striking Force was, it did have vulnerabilities and these were displayed during the Indian Ocean operation.

In March 1942, most of the Striking Force was able to stand down from operations. The original date for Operation C to commence was 21 March with the first air strike against targets on Ceylon scheduled for 1 April. This was delayed by the requirement to keep some of the Striking Force in home waters to protect the homeland from potential American carrier raids. On 4 March, Marcus Island was attacked by USN carrier aircraft and in response the 5th Carrier Division was held in home waters. It was released on 7 March and on 8 March it departed Japan for Staring Bay in the Dutch East Indies.

Soryu, pictured in April 1938, was the first Japanese fleet carrier designed from the keel up as such. With a large air group on a fairly small hull, *Soryu* epitomized the IJN's emphasis on offensive capabilities. (Yamato Museum)

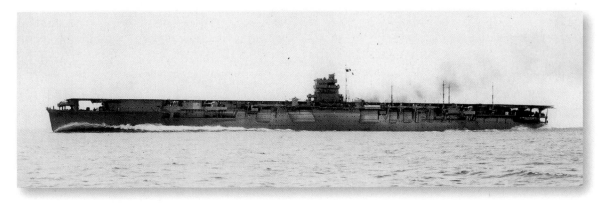

This photo of *Hiryu* dates from June 1938 when the carrier was conducting final sea trials. As a modified design from its near-sister *Soryu*, *Hiryu* provided the basis for all subsequent Japanese fleet carrier designs. (Yamato Museum)

However, on 10 March a USN carrier force was assessed to be north of Wake Island based on communications intelligence. The assessment was faulty, but it prompted the recall of the 5th Carrier Division. It was not released to resume its transit to Staring Bay until 15 March. This forced a delay to Operation C on 17 March. On that date the Combined Fleet changed the start of the operation to 26 March with the first attack on Ceylon scheduled for 5 April.

At full strength, the Striking Force consisted of three carrier divisions, each with two carriers. However, the only time the Striking Force employed all six fleet carriers in a single operation was the Pearl Harbor attack. The Indian Ocean operation used five carriers, the second highest total after Pearl Harbor.

The 1st Carrier Division was comprised of carriers *Akagi* and *Kaga*. As a converted battlecruiser and battleship, respectively, they were the largest carriers in the Striking Force. *Akagi* displayed 36,500 tons standard displacement, was capable of 31 knots and had an aircraft capacity of 66. It was Nagumo's flagship. *Kaga* was not available for Operation C having touched an uncharted rock at Palau on 9 February. On 13 March, it was scrubbed from participation in Operation C and two days later departed Staring Bay and headed to Sasebo for permanent repairs.

The 2nd Carrier Division included the IJN's first two fleet carriers designed as such from the keel up. *Soryu* was completed in 1938, followed by its near-sister ship *Hiryu* in 1939. Both epitomized the Japanese preference for a carrier capable of fast speed (34 knots) and able to carry a large air group for maximum offensive potential. Built to treaty limitations that restricted their tonnage, both were not well protected, though *Hiryu*'s design added 1,400 tons of displacement to improve protection and stability. *Soryu* had an aircraft capacity of 63, and *Hiryu* could embark 57 aircraft.

The IJN considered *Hiryu* to be a successful design and used it as the departure point for the succeeding Shokaku class. Both *Shokaku* and *Zuikaku* were completed in 1941 and together comprised the 5th Carrier Division. These were the best carriers in the world until the advent of the USN's Essex class in 1943. Both ships were well protected, capable of 34 knots, possessed high endurance and could embark 72 aircraft. Being the newest of the Striking Force's carriers, they embarked the least-trained air groups and were therefore not seen as being as capable as the fleet's older carriers. The 5th Carrier Division was late rejoining the Striking Force, only arriving at Staring Bay on 24 March. Two days later, the Striking Force departed for the Indian Ocean.

Shokaku pictured in August 1941 after entering service. The Shokaku class was an advanced design created without reference to treaty restrictions with the goal to create a qualitative overmatch against RN and USN carriers in the same way the Yamato class was intended to overwhelm opposing battleships. (Yamato Museum)

The accumulated attrition since December 1941 and low production rates of carrier aircraft reduced the complement of the Striking Force's carriers to below their maximum capacities. A total of 275 aircraft were embarked for Operation C, broken down as follows:

Akagi	54
Soryu	56
Hiryu	54
Shokaku	56
Zuikaku	55

Each of the carriers embarked an air group that was permanently assigned to its parent ship. An air group had three squadrons, each with a normal strength of 18–27 aircraft. The fighter squadron was equipped with the Mitsubishi A6M2 Navy Type 0 Carrier Fighter. Each carrier also had a squadron of what the IJN called carrier attack bombers, or what the USN and RN called torpedo-bombers. The standard Japanese carrier attack bomber of the period was the Nakajima B5N Navy Type 97 Carrier Attack Bomber. Rounding out Japanese air groups was a dive-bomber squadron with the Aichi D3A1 Navy Type 99 Carrier Bomber. The Japanese referred to their dive-bombers as simply carrier bombers.

All these aircraft were very capable by the standards of the period. The Mitsubishi A6M2 Type 0 Carrier Fighter, referred to hereafter as the Zero (as its enemies called it), was the best carrier fighter of its day. By the time of Operation C, it was already a legend. It possessed exceptional manoeuvrability, great climb and acceleration, a relatively strong armament and a top speed of 336mph, combined with unparalleled range. As a dogfighter it was superb, especially if flown by an experienced pilot. However, the mighty Zero was not invincible. Much of its performance was achieved by lightening the airframe as much as possible which meant the aircraft and its pilot were virtually unprotected.

The Nakajima B5N2 Type 97 Carrier Attack Bomber was later given the Allied reporting name of 'Kate', and will be referred to hereafter as such. It was capable of carrying up to 1,764lbs of bombs or the excellent Type 91 torpedo. The Kate's versatility meant it could operate as a torpedo-bomber or as a level bomber against land targets. It was fairly fast at 235mph but only carried a single rear-firing 7.7mm machine gun for self-defence. The

reliable Type 91 torpedo made the Kate a formidable ship-killing platform. Like the Zero, the Kate's weakness was its vulnerability to damage because of its light construction.

Finally, the Aichi D3A1 Type 99 Carrier Bomber was given the Allied reporting name 'Val', and will be referred to as such in this book. Despite its dated appearance by virtue of its fixed landing gear, it was a very stable and effective dive-bomber. In the hands of an experienced pilot, the Val was capable of great accuracy. It proved this by sinking more Allied ships during the war than any other type of Japanese aircraft. It was limited by its relatively light payload (one 551lb bomb on the centreline and two 132lb bombs on the wings) and like other Japanese aircraft it was not well protected.

The key to the Striking Force's power was its ability to conduct large-scale air operations. Instead of each carrier air group flying separate strikes as was the case in the USN and RN, the Striking Force's different carriers and carrier divisions routinely trained and fought together and were capable of mounting synchronized strikes. Typically, each carrier would contribute either its carrier attack bomber or carrier bomber squadron to an attack while preparing the other squadron for a second-wave attack or as a reserve. Escort for the attack was provided by six or nine fighters from each carrier. In this manner, a large number of aircraft could be launched quickly and combined into a large strike with sufficient numbers to overwhelm enemy defences.

In addition to flying excellent aircraft, Japanese carrier aircrews were generally well-trained and experienced. For three weeks until they departed Staring Bay on 26 March, the aircrews of the 1st and 2nd Carrier Divisions had the opportunity to go ashore to the nearby airfield at Kendari and conduct training. The drills were difficult and according to Japanese sources the skills of the aircrew improved markedly. The aircrews of the 5th Carrier Division were not as highly experienced however and Genda tended to give them secondary responsibilities during his strike planning.

In addition to its core of fleet carriers, the Striking Force included an escort of modern ships. For Operation C, this included all four of the Kongo-class battleships. Of the IJN's ten pre-war battleships, the Kongo class was the only one capable of operating at high speeds that made its ships suitable for escorting the Striking Force. Each Kongo-class ship carried a main battery of eight 14in guns. Despite extensive modernization between the wars, these

Zuikaku shown in the fall of 1941 after it entered service. The addition of the two Shokaku-class carriers greatly augmented the power of the Striking Force immediately before the opening of the war. (Yamato Museum)

Kongo in November 1936 running trials after its virtual rebuild which made it into a fast battleship. Even after this extensive modernization, it was the least well-protected IJN battleship. It would have been outgunned by any of the RN battleships in the Indian Ocean in April 1942. (Yamato Museum)

ships retained fairly weak protection. The 8th Cruiser Division with heavy cruisers *Tone* and *Chikuma* was designed to operate with the carriers. These were modern ships, completed in 1939, and were unique for having their entire main battery of eight 8in guns placed forward. This left the entire after section of the ships for aviation facilities and up to five floatplanes could be carried. The escort was rounded out with a squadron of modern destroyers led by a light cruiser. Japanese destroyers were maximized for torpedo attack and carried up to 16 of the excellent Type 93 torpedo. However, they were much less proficient in anti-submarine or anti-air warfare. None of the ships of the Striking Force carried radar.

Striking Force doctrine called for reconnaissance duties to be performed by floatplanes from the escorts. This was done to keep as many of the Kates (the carrier aircraft best suited for search missions) available for attack missions. This was another manifestation of how offensively minded the IJN was. The problem with this doctrine was the low number and short range of the floatplanes carried by the escorting battleships and cruisers. Each battleship carried three floatplanes while *Tone* and *Chikuma* carried five; with *Abukuma*'s single floatplane the Striking Force's total was 23 floatplanes. Eighteen of these were the E8N2 Type 95 (Allied reporting name 'Dave') with a clearly inadequate search range of about 200nm and low cruising speed of about 100 knots. Because of their numbers, they were the Striking Force's primary search aircraft. Only three of the old E7K2 Type 94 ('Alf') floatplanes were available; they had a greater endurance than the Type 95. The best Japanese reconnaissance floatplane was the Aichi E13A Navy Type 0 Reconnaissance Seaplane ('Jake'). First introduced in 1940, this was an excellent aircraft with a maximum speed of some 200 knots and endurance of almost 15 hours. However, only two were available for Operation C with one each embarked on *Chikuma* and *Tone*. The Japanese ambivalence regarding search operations is hard to understand. They recognized that good reconnaissance was critical to get the all-important first strike against enemy carriers but were unwilling to properly resource search operations.

As excellent as the Striking Force was offensively, it was much less capable in fleet air defence. The primary means of providing fleet air defence was by mounting standing combat air patrols (CAP). Typically, half of the

carriers' 18-Zero fighter squadron was devoted to fleet air defence. The lack of radar made early warning dependent on the small standing number of fighters on CAP or from one of the escort ships. Early warning was key to giving the remaining Zeros a chance to scramble to meet incoming threats. Though the Zero had the capability to quickly climb to interception altitude, the potential lack of early warning was a critical weakness. Once the Zero was airborne, its lack of a reliable radio made airborne direction all but impossible. Added to the potential weakness of the CAP was the marginal capabilities of Japanese anti-aircraft weapons. The standard long-range anti-aircraft gun was the Type 89 5in High-Angle Gun which was handicapped by poor fire control directors. This placed the emphasis of shipborne air defence on the ubiquitous Type 96 25mm gun. This was a mediocre weapon in all respects, and its fire control director was also incapable of handling high-speed targets.

Both of the Tone-class heavy cruisers were assigned to the Combined Fleet's carrier force for the majority of their careers. This is *Chikuma* in 1941. Note the four floatplanes aft. (Yamato Museum)

The Malaya Unit Striking Force

Vice Admiral Ozawa's Malaya Unit Striking Force was built around the light carrier *Ryujo*. It was an unsuccessful design built to circumvent treaty restrictions. Designed to carry up to 48 aircraft, it typically carried about 30. For Operation C it carried 29 aircraft divided into 12 older fighters (A5M4 Type 96 'Claude') and 17 Kates. *Ryujo* was unable to operate large numbers of aircraft because of its small flight deck and poor elevator placement. The same limitations precluded launching large strikes.

Five heavy cruisers were also assigned to Ozawa's force. Four of these were the excellent Mogami class. These were large ships displacing over 15,000 tons at full load with a maximum speed of 35 knots, good protection, and a heavy main battery of ten 8in guns. The last heavy cruiser was Ozawa's flagship Chokai with comparable characteristics to the Mogami class. All the cruisers carried three floatplanes.

BRITISH

The Eastern Fleet

Entering the war, much of the RN was old and did not compare favourably with the IJN. Rearmament, begun in 1937, had begun to change the composition of the RN, but this was counterbalanced by the fact that the RN was stretched very thin by worldwide commitments in early 1942. It was fighting in the Atlantic against U-boats and the threat of German surface raiders, engaged in the Mediterranean against the Italians and Germans, had just taken on the added burden of escorting high-priority convoys to Russia through the Norwegian and Barents Sea, and now was faced with a new opponent in the east – the formidable IJN. Before the Japanese opened the war in December 1941, defence of the Far East was the RN's lowest priority. As the Japanese rolled though the Dutch East Indies, Malaya, Singapore and Burma, and now posed a direct threat to the British position in the Indian Ocean, the RN was forced to massively reinforce its Eastern Fleet.

It was planned that units from the Mediterranean Fleet would deploy to the Far East and base at Singapore in the event of Japanese aggression. By late 1941, as war in the Far East loomed, the Mediterranean Fleet was at a low ebb. This meant it took much longer to create a fleet for deployment to the Far East. This was not done in time to save Singapore, but by the spring of 1942, the RN had assembled a large force on the Indian Ocean. This was the fleet that faced the IJN in April 1942.

The Eastern Fleet of April 1942 was not the massive and capable force envisioned by the Admiralty. It totalled 29 ships with less than 100 carrier-based aircraft. On paper, the fleet seemed impressive with its five battleships, three aircraft carriers, seven cruisers and 14 destroyers. The reality however was very different. The Eastern Fleet contained few modern ships, and those that were available had never worked together.

Recognizing the disparate composition of the Eastern Fleet, Somerville divided it into two sections. Force A consisted of the two modern carriers, *Warspite* and the most modern cruisers, and six destroyers. Force B was centred around the light carrier *Hermes*, four Royal Sovereign-class battleships and the older three cruisers, and eight destroyers. Both forces operated together in spite of the slow speed and low endurance of the battleships assigned to Force B. These battleships were a massive encumbrance and provided little value. Presumably, Somerville kept them near the carriers in Force A as insurance if the fast Kongo-class battleships threatened the carriers. The smarter course of action would have been to leave the older battleships in a safe harbour, thus reducing the Eastern Fleet's vulnerability and increasing its flexibility.

British Naval Air Power

A major weakness of the RN was its lack of air power. British naval air power was handicapped by the marked numerical weakness of its carrier aircraft and perhaps even more importantly by the qualitative weakness of the aircraft that were available. This was due in large part to the fact that the RAF dominated air policy, strategy and aircraft procurement. Until 1937, the RAF and the RN laboured under a dual-control system for equipping the carrier fleet with aircraft; the RAF's priority for carrier aircraft was low. It was not until 1939 that the RN gained full control for equipping the

Fleet Air Arm (FAA). By this point, the British had fallen far behind in the development of carrier aircraft and the RN still remained dependent on the Air Ministry for aircraft procurement. By the start of the war, and into the spring of 1942, British naval air power was in no position to compete with the IJN. Despite its handicaps, the RN was advanced in its thinking about the application of carrier air power. It had conducted multi-carrier operations earlier in the war, conducted strikes against enemy fleet in harbour and had a wealth of experience operating carriers under an enemy air threat.

The best RN fighter present in the battle was the Grumman Martlet. Using tactics suited to its strengths, it could compete with the Zero. However, only a single squadron of 12 aircraft was available. (Royal Navy, now in the Public Domain)

With one exception, the aircraft aboard the carriers of the Eastern Fleet were inferior to their Japanese counterparts. The best aircraft was the Grumman Martlet which was the slightly modified RN version of the USN's standard carrier fighter the Grumman F4F Wildcat. The Martlet/Wildcat was respected by the RN which assessed it to be the best carrier fighter in the world during this period. It possessed a top speed comparable to the Zero but was much less manoeuvrable. However, it was a very rugged aircraft with a good armament. If flown with the right tactics, it could better the Zero.

Another fighter in FAA service was the Fairey Fulmar which first entered fleet service in 1940. It was not as bad a fighter as is believed, but it was inferior to the Zero in speed and manoeuvrability. It was much more able to take damage than the Zero and had the speed to catch the Val and Kate. It could achieve high speed in a dive (400mph) to escape from a dogfight if necessary. It was suited to intercepting low-flying and relatively slow torpedo-bombers, but against Japanese dive-bombers it had little advantage. As a CAP aircraft it had the advantages of a four-hour endurance, and a large ammunition capability.

Because of the inadequate numbers of FAA fighters available, the RAF's Hurricane was adapted for carrier use. While a capable fighter, the resulting Sea Hurricane was not really suitable for carrier duties. It lacked folding wings, and therefore could only use the forward elevators found on Illustrious-class carriers. It also had a very short endurance.

Unlike the IJN (and the USN) which developed dedicated torpedo-bombers and dive-bombers, the FAA used a single aircraft for reconnaissance, bombing and torpedo missions. This was the Fairey Swordfish Mk I which first flew in 1934. By 1942, it was clearly obsolete with its slow speed, short range and weak defensive armament. The replacement for the Swordfish was the Albacore, also designed by Fairey. It first flew in 1938 and by 1942 was the standard strike aircraft aboard RN fleet carriers. It was not much of an improvement since it was still a dated biplane design with a top speed of 161mph. However, it was a versatile aircraft being able to perform several roles, including level bomber, dive-bomber, torpedo-bomber, reconnaissance and spotting for naval gunfire. It had a short strike range, usually 100nm.

The best RN strike aircraft present in the battle was the Fairey Albacore. This is a *Formidable* Albacore pictured with a torpedo. The Albacore was a capable torpedo-bomber but against the Japanese could only operate at night. (Royal Navy, now in the Public Domain)

Without fighter cover, the Albacore would be at the mercy of intercepting Zeros. To overcome this significant limitation, the RN preferred to employ the Albacore at night or in bad weather. The aircrews were trained to operate in these conditions. The Albacores on *Formidable* carried the ASV 2 surface-search radar. This was a new device having been first deployed in early 1941 and had an effective range of 15–20nm depending on the size of the target. The standard RN air-launched torpedo was the Mark XII introduced in 1940. It could be dropped from up to 200ft and at speeds of up to 150 knots. Though nowhere as powerful as the strike aircraft on Japanese carriers, the Albacore could be effective under the right conditions.

Unlike the air groups found on Japanese carriers, the two RN fleet carriers embarked non-standard air groups. *Indomitable* had four squadrons aboard. The two fighter squadrons included one with nine Sea Hurricane IBs and the second with 12 Fulmar IIs. The two strike squadrons operated 24 Albacores between them. The carrier had been employed as a Hurricane ferry to the Dutch East Indies and Ceylon during which it had to disembark two of its squadrons. This meant there was no training time before it joined the Eastern Fleet in mid-March.

Formidable arrived at Colombo on 24 March. It embarked a totally green air group that had to work up on the transit from the United Kingdom. The single fighter squadron was equipped with 12 Martlet IIs and was considered reasonably proficient. The two strike squadrons were equipped with Albacores and were ASV 2-equipped. The Albacore squadrons had suffered a number of accidents and were not considered well trained.

The third carrier in the Eastern Fleet, *Hermes*, embarked a weak air group with no fighters and an inadequate number (12) of Swordfish to accomplish search and strike missions concurrently. However, this unit possessed combat experience.

Compared to the aircraft they operated, RN fleet carriers were top-notch ships. The most modern of British carriers was the Illustrious class of new armoured fleet carriers. Four ships of this class were under construction at the start of the war. Two of the ships were in the Indian Ocean by April 1942 and made fine additions to the Eastern Fleet. They possessed high speed (30.5 knots) and a good anti-aircraft battery of 16 4.5in guns and six eight-barrel pom-poms. Their best feature was their armoured flight deck which made them somewhat immune to high-level and dive-bombing. However, the design sacrificed aircraft capacity. *Formidable* was capable of carrying about 36 aircraft, or about two-thirds that of a Japanese fleet carrier.

Indomitable was the first carrier assigned to the Eastern Fleet, and was the fourth unit of the Illustrious class. It retained the armoured flight deck, but a reduction of the side armour meant it was fitted with another hangar deck increasing aircraft capacity to 48. Completed in October 1941, it was the best RN carrier afloat in the spring of 1942. Both fleet carriers were fitted with the Type 79 radar which was capable of detecting a target at 10,000ft at some 60nm.

Hermes was a familiar presence in the Far East. This is the RN's first purpose-built carrier pictured off the Chinese coast in 1931 with its unmistakable large island. By 1942, its slow speed and small aircraft capacity made it a second-line unit. (Naval History and Heritage Command)

Hermes was definitely a second-line unit having been launched in 1924 as the RN's first carrier designed as such from the keel up. It was slow for a fleet carrier – 25 knots – and thus had problems launching fully laden aircraft without the help of a steady wind. Its aircraft capacity was 12 Swordfish.

The RN sent a significant proportion of its battleship fleet to the Far East in the early part of the Pacific War. The first British capital ships to see action against the Japanese were *Prince of Wales* and *Repulse*. Both arrived in Singapore just before the start of the war and were immediately taken to sea by Admiral Phillips to attack Japanese invasion convoys. There were no invasion convoys to attack, but a land-based Japanese air unit found and sank both ships on 10 December. This was a shock of the first order to the RN. *Repulse* was a World War I design which had been little

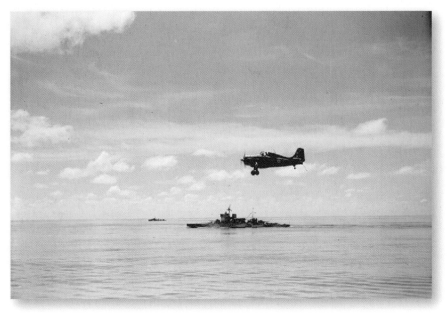

Somerville's flagship was the battleship *Warspite*, shown here during the timeframe of the Indian Ocean raid with a Martlet in the foreground overhead. *Warspite* had been extensively modernized before the war and was later fitted with radar. It was the most powerful battleship in the Indian Ocean during this period. (Royal Navy, now in the Public Domain)

modernized between the wars, but *Prince of Wales* was the most modern British battleship available. It had been sunk by Japanese aircraft that the RN so easily dismissed as incapable of such a feat.

The Eastern Fleet boasted five battleships. Somerville's flagship during the operation was the modernized *Warspite*. It was a Queen Elizabeth-class battleship built during World War I but had been thoroughly modernized between 1934 and 1937. It emerged with increased protection and a much improved anti-aircraft fit. With its 15in main battery and excellent protection, it was more than a match for any of the Japanese battleships involved in Operation C. Its main weakness was its top speed of 24 knots which made it slower than its Japanese counterparts.

The bulk of Somerville's battle force was comprised of the four remaining Royal Sovereign-class battleships. These had also been completed during World War I but had not been extensively modernized between the wars. *Revenge* was in the Indian Ocean when the war began, and *Royal Sovereign* was planned to arrive in Singapore by the end of December. *Ramillies* and *Resolution* left Britain in early January 1942 for the Far East. All four ships received minor improvements in protection and to their anti-aircraft fit before departing. *Resolution* and *Royal Sovereign* had their 15in guns equipped for supercharged firing which extended their range to 28,732 yards with the latest shells. These ships formed the 3rd Battle Squadron under Rear Admiral Bonham-Carter.

However, these ships were deficient in underwater protection and possessed a severe lack of anti-aircraft protection. Worst of all, they were slow – they could make a maximum speed of 21 knots. They also possessed low endurance. Not being designed for operations in tropical waters, they had to be replenished with water every 3–4 days. On the positive side, they did carry a main battery of eight 15in guns. This was a heavier broadside than any of the Kongo-class battleships. Given their limitations, it is difficult to understand what role the R-class could play in a modern strike force.

Launched in 1926, *Cornwall* was a member of the RN's first class of treaty cruisers. These County-class heavy cruisers featured a main battery of eight 8in guns and a long hull with a high freeboard to assist in speed and seaworthiness. The design did not emphasize protection and the ships' armoured deck was too thin to be effective against air attack. (Naval History and History Command)

Modern RN cruisers were in desperately short supply in the spring of 1942, and this showed in the Eastern Fleet. The best of the lot were two County-class heavy cruisers, *Cornwall* and *Dorsetshire*, but the latter was undergoing refit in Colombo. It cut short the refit and joined the fleet on the afternoon of 1 April. These treaty cruisers did not compare well to their IJN counterparts carrying only eight 8in guns, being capable of only 31 knots and possessing less protection. Light cruisers *Emerald* and *Enterprise* were also old, but with their high speed and modern radar, they were potentially good ships for night attacks. The three light cruisers allocated to Force B were of very limited value. *Caledon* and *Dragon* were commissioned in World War I, and Dutch *Jacob van Heemskerck* carried only 4in guns.

Another weakness was the lack of modern destroyers. In the spring of 1942, only the bare minimum was available to provide for the Eastern Fleet. The best six – *Napier*, *Nestor*, *Paladin*, *Panther*, *Hotspur* and *Foxhound* – were assigned to Force A. *Napier* and *Nestor* were operated by the Royal Australian Navy. These ships carried a mix of 4in and 4.7in guns and between four and ten torpedo tubes. Only two were less than seven years old and all had very limited anti-aircraft capabilities. The eight destroyers assigned to Force B were similarly armed but were all older with two dating back to World War I. They suffered from a variety of reliability issues.

For the entire Eastern Fleet, protection against enemy air attack was a major weakness. The best method of defence was with fighters, but only a small number were available. All the available fighters lacked a high rate of climb, so to protect against high-level or dive-bomber attack, the British had to maintain a standing CAP. However, the RN did have the massive advantage of radar and had some experience in using radar in guiding fighters against incoming threats.

Generally speaking, even by early 1942 RN ships were unable to defend themselves against concerted air attack relying on their own anti-aircraft defences. The RN's high-altitude control system (HACS) used to direct anti-aircraft fire was based on estimation of the target's location, not on measurement of its actual movement. Even the flawed HACS was effective against aircraft flying at a predictable altitude and speed, but this was not

Dorsetshire, launched in 1929, was an improved County-class heavy cruiser. In this view, the catapult fitted in 1932–33 is clearly visible. The ship also received radar and had a fine record including a prominent role in the sinking of German battleship *Bismarck* in May 1941. However, its horizontal protection was inadequate. (Naval History and History Command)

the flight profile of IJN dive-bombers and torpedo-bombers. In particular, the RN was vulnerable to dive-bombing as early war experience against the Germans had demonstrated. Torpedo-bombers could be dealt with by a large number of smaller anti-aircraft guns (40mm and 20mm), but these lacked the effective range to destroy a torpedo-bomber before it had an opportunity to launch its weapon.

The RN had a wide array of anti-aircraft guns during this period of the war. Long-range anti-aircraft weapons included the 4in, 4.5in, two types of 4.7in and the modern 5.25in. Some of these lacked the elevation to deal with dive-bombers, and even the 5.25in gun was too slow in training speed and rate of fire. The mainstay intermediate range weapon was the 2-pdr multi-barrel pom-pom dating from the 1920s. This came in four-barrel and eight-barrel variants, depending on the size of ship. The effective 20mm Oerlikon was coming into service but was not yet universally available.

Intelligence

Allied intelligence played a vital role in the battle. In general, the RN underrated the IJN before the war. The British believed the IJN would be a cautious opponent and was rated at only 80 per cent as efficient as the RN. The underestimation of IJN air power was the biggest problem. The British understood the basics of the IJN's carrier fleet and its aircraft but failed to 'connect the dots' to develop an understanding of how carrier air power would become so dominant when employed by the Japanese. As IJN doctrine for carrier air power evolved, the British failed to recognize it. To be fair, the Americans also failed to understand how much progress Japanese carrier doctrine had advanced in the months before the war. When it came to the tactical dimensions of Japanese carrier air power, the British still got it wrong. They continually underestimated the aircraft capacity of Japanese carriers. They expected those carriers to carry strike aircraft like the Swordfish. Somerville and his staff were also surprised by the appearance of 'fighter bombers' to sink two British cruisers on 5 April when intelligence was available on the IJN's standard dive-bombers which were actually responsible.

In the area of operational intelligence, the RN had a significant advantage. Though the British had the immense advantage of knowing the Japanese plan before the Striking Force entered the Indian Ocean, this was not used to best advantage. Knowing the Japanese were coming saved the Eastern Fleet from any possibility of being 'Pearl Harbored' in Colombo, but failure to use the high-grade intelligence correctly almost led to disaster.

Both the British and Americans were attacking the IJN's primary operational code, named JN 25 by the Allies. Efforts to penetrate JN 25 pre-war resulted in no operational intelligence, but after the war began both the Americans and British made significant progress into JN 25B, which had been introduced in December 1940.

When it came to Japanese plans for Operation C, the British enjoyed a high degree of insight into Japanese intentions. The Far East Combined Bureau (FECB) was the RN's codebreaking organization focused on the IJN. It had relocated from Singapore to Ceylon. Working with the Americans, the FECB had continued to make progress in its efforts to penetrate JN 25B in the first few months of 1942. Its ability to read large segments of JN 25B was demonstrated around 20 March when a series of messages were

intercepted and decrypted enough to paint a picture of Operation C. The decrypts revealed that a Japanese carrier force would leave Staring Bay on 21 March to conduct operations in the 'D' Area (assessed to be Ceylon) with an air strike scheduled against 'DG' (assessed to be Colombo) on 2 April. In addition to the carrier force, a force comprised of heavy cruisers would also be active in the Indian Ocean.

Somerville and his staff examined the assessments of FECB in a conference on 29 March. The results of the session were summarized for the Admiralty in a message sent later that day. The results of the conference showed both the benefits and pitfalls of intelligence. As was always the case, the decrypts of JN 25B did not provide total insight into Japanese plans. The gaps were filled by inference and interpretation, and of course these were not always accurate.

While Somerville accepted FECB's assessment that a major Japanese operation into the Indian Ocean was pending, the British drew false conclusions about the date of the operation and the strength of the Japanese forces conducting it. Based on the decryptions, the size of the Japanese force was assessed to be two carriers, four cruisers and 12 destroyers. The attack on Ceylon would occur on or about 1 April. After the air attack, the carrier force would be supported by battleships. The size of the carrier force (only two carriers) suggested to Somerville that the Japanese were conducting a hit-and-run raid. A raid by only two carriers was a misleading and important assessment. The Eastern Fleet had a chance against a two-carrier force but would be in total jeopardy against Nagumo's actual five-carrier force.

Obviously the two-carrier assessment was a gross error that almost led to disaster. There were other intelligence entities that painted a much different, and ultimately more accurate, picture. The USN shared its daily intelligence assessment of IJN ship locations with the FECB and the Admiralty. The RN's Naval Intelligence Division (NID) provided a weekly assessment of

The best of the RN's old light cruisers in service in 1942 was the two-ship E class. Both *Emerald* and *Enterprise* were assigned to the Eastern Fleet in April 1942. This is *Emerald* in a pre-war photograph. By 1942, it carried six 6in guns, had been equipped with radar and retained a top speed of 33 knots. Both ships in the class were lightly protected. (Naval History and History Command)

IJN locations and intentions. The NID assessed that the Japanese were more likely to use at least three carriers in any Indian Ocean operations with three Kongo-class battleships and many cruisers. This larger force was more in keeping with the recent record of Japanese carrier force attacks, as evinced by the Pearl Harbor, Rabaul and Darwin operations. The Admiralty was in a good position to understand the broad scope of Japanese intentions in the Indian Ocean even if Somerville was not. It should have cautioned Somerville after learning of his 29 March assessment of Japanese force levels earmarked for Operation C. Failure to do so almost allowed Somerville to blunder his way into a major disaster.

Typical of the destroyers assigned to the Eastern Fleet's Force A was the N Class. Launched in 1940–41, they were well-armed with three twin 4.7in mounts and one bank of torpedoes. Four of the eight ships in the class were manned by the Royal Australian Navy including *Nestor*, shown here in the Indian Ocean during the timeframe of the Indian Ocean raid. (Royal Navy, now in the Public Domain)

Just as critical was the British inability to track the developments that led the Japanese to delay their attack on Ceylon from the original 1 April date to 5 April. Somerville acted on the signals intelligence with the original 1 April attack date, but when the attack failed to develop as predicted he assessed that the intelligence was incorrect in its entirety. In fact, the attack was just delayed. This ensuing confusion resulted in many British casualties.

Air Forces

Even though the British service chiefs realized that air power was key in the defence of the region, higher priorities kept the number of aircraft earmarked for the Indian Ocean to a minimum. By March 1942, defence of Ceylon was given a top priority and air reinforcements were flowing to the island.

The first air units to arrive on the island were two Fleet Air Arm squadrons equipped with Fulmar II fighters. These were 803 and 806 Squadrons with an original strength of 24 aircraft. At China Bay, 273 Squadron was established with Seal and Vildebeest biplanes and some Fulmar I and II fighters from the FAA. Additional Fulmars arrived in late March to bring the unit up to a strength of 16 fighters.

The principal British fighter on Ceylon was the Hurricane. Compared to the Zero, it possessed a comparable top speed and was better armed; however, it compared poorly in manoeuvrability and rate of climb. Adopted for carrier use, it became the Sea Hurricane as shown in this photo. (Public Domain)

The best British fighter in the Far East during this period was the Hurricane. Strengthening the air defence of the island meant getting more Hurricanes there as quickly as possible. The first Hurricanes arrived from Karachi on 23 February. In early March, 30 and 261 Squadrons with Hurricanes were flown in from carrier *Indomitable* – 30 Squadron was a veteran unit; 261 Squadron had limited operational experience. Later in March, 258 Squadron was formed with Hurricanes flown by aviators from various sources, some with combat

experience. Two of the Hurricane squadrons were based at Colombo and the third was stationed at Trincomalee.

Lack of strike aircraft on Ceylon was a salient weakness. No modern torpedo-bombers (like the Beaufort) were available, nor were any Wellington long-range bombers. The only strike aircraft on Ceylon was a squadron of Blenheim light bombers. This was 11 Squadron which had arrived at Ratmalana on 15 March with 14 Blenheim IV light bombers. The Blenheim IV was relatively slow, carried a weak defensive armament and carried only bombs. This unit had seen action in the Western Desert but was totally untrained to attack maritime targets. Added to the RAF's bomber squadron was 788 Squadron of Swordfish biplane torpedo-bombers flown by the FAA.

A critical requirement for the defence of Ceylon was long-range reconnaissance aircraft. By the time the Japanese struck, there were only eight Catalina flying boats available; three from 240 Squadron, one each from 202 and 205 Squadrons, and three from 413 (Canadian) Squadron which had begun to arrive on 28 March. Of these, six were operational. There were also four Dutch Catalinas, survivors of the NEI campaign, but they were unserviceable.

In early April, British air strength on Ceylon had been built up to almost 140 aircraft. This included 54 Hurricanes, 40 Fulmar IIs, 2 Martlets, 14 Blenheims, 16 Swordfish and 12 Catalina flying boats. However, not all of these were operational. Despite the significant air reinforcement to Ceylon before the Japanese attack, the British were not in a favourable position to handle the massed air power that the Striking Force could bring to bear. While the Hurricane was a fairly modern fighter, it was still inferior to the Zero and was flown by mostly inexperienced pilots. The Fulmar was in no way comparable to the Zero and was also flown by few pilots with combat experience. It could though exact a toll on Japanese bombers if given the chance. The British were particularly deficient in striking power with only a handful of Swordfish that could not operate in daylight against fighter opposition and a single squadron of Blenheims whose crews had no training or experience attacking maritime targets. The Catalina force was too small to mount continuous searches around the island, but it would perform well in the coming battle.

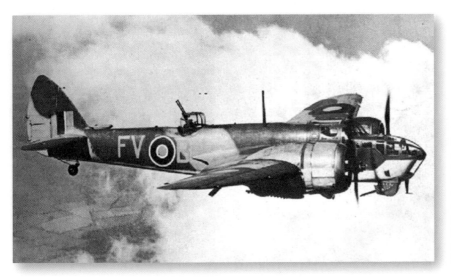

The only RAF strike aircraft on Ceylon were the Blenheim IVs of 11 Squadron. This aircraft was unsuited to maritime strikes; in addition, the lack of training of the aircrews in conducting this mission meant the British had almost no ability to attack Japanese naval forces using air forces from Ceylon. (Author's collection)

Facilities

Throughout 1942, the Eastern Fleet suffered from a lack of proper facilities. The two naval ports on Ceylon, Colombo and Trincomalee, were not well developed. Neither had repair facilities or a dry dock capable of handling large ships. They were only adequate as refuelling stations and anchorages. The British realized that these facilities were known to the Japanese and thus were vulnerable to potential attack. To avoid this, the RN developed a new 'secret' base called Port T. This was located at Addu Atoll in the southern Maldives some 600nm south-west of Colombo. Work on the base had begun in the autumn of 1941 but by early 1942 it only provided an anchorage with the ability to supply fuel and water. Defences at the base were marginal and there was no airfield. Nevertheless, the existence of Port T was unknown to the Japanese and it would be heavily used in April 1942.

There were few operational airfields on Ceylon in April 1942. Near Trincomalee was a large field known as China Bay. Ratmalana Airfield was the main air facility in Colombo. To alleviate crowding at this facility, the British converted the Colombo racecourse into an airfield. This was unknown to the Japanese. Also unknown to the Japanese was the satellite airfield at Kokkilai some 35nm north-west of China Bay. The Catalina flying boats flew from Koggala, a small lake on the south coast.

ORDERS OF BATTLE

JAPANESE

STRIKING FORCE

Vice Admiral Nagumo
Air Raid Unit
1st Air Fleet
1st Carrier Division (Nagumo)
 Carrier *Akagi*:
 Akagi Fighter Squadron – 19 Zeros
 Akagi Carrier Bomber Squadron – 17 Vals
 Akagi Carrier Attack Bomber Squadron – 18 Kates
2nd Carrier Division (Rear Admiral Yamaguchi Tamon)
 Carrier *Hiryu*:
 Hiryu Fighter Squadron – 18 Zeros
 Hiryu Carrier Bomber Squadron – 18 Vals
 Hiryu Carrier Attack Bomber Squadron – 18 Kates
 Carrier *Soryu*:
 Soryu Fighter Squadron – 20 Zeros
 Soryu Carrier Bomber Squadron – 18 Vals
 Soryu Carrier Attack Bomber Squadron – 18 Kates
5th Carrier Division (Rear Admiral Hara Chuichi)
 Carrier *Shokaku*:
 Shokaku Fighter Squadron – 18 Zeros
 Shokaku Carrier Bomber Squadron – 19 Vals
 Shokaku Carrier Attack Bomber Squadron – 19 Kates
 Carrier *Zuikaku*:
 Zuikaku Fighter Squadron – 18 Zeros
 Zuikaku Carrier Bomber Squadron – 19 Vals
 Zuikaku Carrier Attack Bomber Squadron – 18 Kates
Total: 275 aircraft
Support Unit
Battleships *Kongo*, *Kirishima*, *Haruna* and *Hiei* from 3rd Battleship Division (with 12 Dave floatplanes)
Heavy cruisers *Tone* and *Chikuma* from 8th Cruiser Division (with two Jake, two Alf and six Dave floatplanes)

Guard Unit
1st Destroyer Squadron
 Light Cruiser *Abukuma* (with one Alf floatplane)
 17th Destroyer Division – destroyers *Hamakaze*, *Isokaze*, *Tanikaze*, *Urakaze*
 18th Destroyer Division – destroyers *Arare*, *Kagero*, *Kasumi*, *Shiranui*
 4th Destroyer Division, 2nd Section
 Destroyer *Akigumo*
Supply Unit
1st Supply Division – oilers *Shinkoku Maru*, *Kenyo Maru*, *Nippon Maru*, *Toei Maru*
2nd Supply Division – oilers *Nichiro Maru*, *Toei Maru No. 2*, *Hoyo Maru*

MALAYA UNIT STRIKING FORCE

Vice Admiral Ozawa
Centre Unit
Heavy Cruiser *Chokai*
Light cruiser *Yura*
Light carrier *Ryujo* from the 4th Carrier Division
 Ryujo Fighter Squadron – 12 A5M4 Type 96s (Claude)
 Ryujo Carrier Attack Bomber Squadron – 17 Kates
Destroyers *Yugiri* and *Asagiri* from the 20th Destroyer Division
North Unit
Heavy Cruisers *Kumano* and *Suzuya* from the 7th Cruiser Division
Destroyer *Shirakumo* from the 20th Destroyer Division
South Unit
Heavy Cruisers *Mikuma* and *Mogami* from the 7th Cruiser Division
Destroyer *Amagiri* from the 20th Destroyer Division
Supply Unit
Oiler *Nichiei Maru*
Destroyers *Ayanami* and *Shiokaze* (detached from 4th Carrier Division)
Guard Unit
3rd Destroyer Squadron
Light Cruiser *Sendai*

11th Destroyer Division and 1st Section of the 19th Destroyer
    Division
    Destroyers *Hatsuyuki, Shirayuki, Fubuki, Murakumo, Uranami,
    Isonami*

SUBMARINE UNIT

Submarine Unit C (Rear Admiral Ichioka Hisashi)
    Submarines *I-2, I-3, I-4, I-5, I-6, I-7*

BRITISH FORCES

EASTERN FLEET

Force A (Fast class)
Fleet carriers:
Indomitable
    800 Squadron – 12 Fulmar IIs
    880 Squadron – 9 Sea Hurricane IBs
    827 Squadron – 12 Albacores
    831 Squadron – 12 Albacores
Formidable
    888 Squadron – 12 Martlet IIs
    818 Squadron – 9 Albacores
    820 Squadron – 12 Albacores
Battleship *Warspite*
Heavy cruisers *Cornwall, Dorsetshire*
Light cruisers *Emerald, Enterprise*
Destroyers *Foxhound, Hotspur, Napier, Nestor, Paladin, Panther*

Force B (Slow class)
Light carrier *Hermes*
    814 Squadron – 12 Swordfish
Battleships *Ramillies, Resolution, Revenge, Royal Sovereign*
Light cruisers *Caledon, Dragon, Jacob van Heemskerck* (Royal
    Netherlands Navy)
Destroyers *Arrow, Decoy, Fortune, Griffin, Isaac Sweers* (Royal
    Norwegian Navy), *Norman, Scout, Vampire* (Royal Australian
    Navy)

Air Units on Ceylon
In Colombo Area
Ratmalana Airfield
    30 Squadron – 22 Hurricane IIBs
    803 Squadron (FAA) – 12 Fulmar IIs
    806 Squadron (FAA) – 12 Fulmar IIs
Racecourse Airfield
    258 Squadron – 9 Hurricane IIBs, 5 Hurricane IBs
    11 Squadron – 14 Blenheim IVs
Anti-aircraft guns:
    20 3.7in guns
    4 3in guns
    35 40mm Bofors
One radar

Koggala Lagoon
202 Squadron – one Catalina
205 Squadron – one Catalina
240 Squadron – three Catalina
413 Squadron (RCAF) – three Catalina
(Of these, only six were operational)

In Trincomalee Area
261 Squadron RAF – 17 Hurricane IIBs and one Hurricane I
273 Squadron RAF – 16 Fulmar Is/IIs
Two Martlets from *Indomitable*
788 Squadron FAA – six Swordfish
814 Squadron FAA was based on *Hermes*, but on the day of the
    Japanese attack was ashore at China Bay with 10 Swordfish Is.
    The other two aircraft of the squadron were on the carrier under
    repair.
Anti-aircraft guns:
    20 3.7in anti-aircraft guns
    34 40mm Bofors anti-aircraft guns
One radar at Elizabeth Point, north of Trincomalee

OPPOSING PLANS

JAPANESE

Despite the weakness of the British in the Indian Ocean, the Japanese never made any serious plans to mount a major offensive in the region. There was no serious coordination with the Germans regarding operations in the Indian Ocean, and any major offensive would require cooperation between the IJN and the IJA. In February 1942, the two services held a war game to examine a Ceylon operation of which neither service was a proponent. The IJA lacked the forces for the initial attack or to garrison the island after its capture. For its part, the IJN was also reluctant since it needed all available ships for Phase Two operations in the Pacific. Above all, logistical concerns made any Ceylon operation a pipe dream. The Japanese simply lacked the shipping required to move a large force deep into the Indian Ocean and then keep it supplied in the face of what would likely be persistent British submarine, air and even surface attack. In early March, Premier Tojo Hideki ruled out an Indian Ocean operation for the present time.

Even though a massive offensive into the region was ruled out, the Japanese were already making plans to expand into the Indian Ocean region even before the conquest of the southern resource areas was complete. Planning for this next phase of operations began on 14 February, the day before the fall of Singapore. By 21 February, the Southern Army Commander General Terauchi Hisaichi and Vice Admiral Ozawa reached an agreement. As soon as mine clearance in the Strait of Malacca had been accomplished, a sequence of operations would begin. Mine clearing was scheduled to be complete by the end of February or the beginning or March. Operation *T*, the landing of troops in northern Sumatra to complete the conquest of that island, would be conducted first. At about 20 days after the completion of mine clearing operations, the invasion of the Andaman Islands (Operation *D*) and the movement of IJA forces to Burma (Operation *U*) would commence. Operation *U* entailed the movement of two divisions from Singapore and Penang to Rangoon. A prerequisite for Operations *D* and *U* was moving IJN land-based air units to Bangkok to provide cover.

The movement of British naval forces into the Indian Ocean region posed potential risks to Operations *D* and *U*. Therefore, the Navy General Staff and the Combined Fleet studied and agreed to the feasibility of mounting a surprise attack against the British fleet in Ceylon. To conduct this operation, the Striking Force, which was already in the region supporting the last phase

of the conquest of the Dutch East Indies, was retained under the Southern Task Force and ordered to conduct the operation into the Indian Ocean.

On 9 March, Yamamoto gave Southern Task Force commander Vice Admiral Kondo the orders to carry out the attack on Ceylon. The date of the operation was set for the period from mid-March to early April. The mission of the Striking Force was nothing less than attacking the Royal Navy's Eastern Fleet and destroying it. In IJN parlance, the raid was a 'manoeuvring operation'.

Concurrent with the plans devised by the Navy General Staff and the Combined Fleet to employ the Striking Force to destroy British naval power in the Indian Ocean, Malaya Unit Commander Vice Admiral Ozawa was working on an independent plan to use the surface ships of his Malaya Unit to conduct a foray into the northern Bay of Bengal to attack the SLOCs to Calcutta. This would also protect the projected Andaman Island operation. After the issuance of the Combined Fleet order on 9 March for the Striking Force attack against Ceylon, Ozawa proposed to Kondo that the Bay of Bengal operation be conducted in concert with the planned attack on Ceylon. After consulting with the Combined Fleet, Kondo agreed on 14 March that the two operations should be synchronized. However, Kondo instructed that the Malaya Unit keep to the northern part of the Bay of Bengal and not advance west of the 85 degrees longitude line until the Striking Force had made its surprise attack.

Japanese intelligence on Allied naval strength in the Indian Ocean was out of date and lacked specifics. As of early March, the RN was assessed to have carriers *Hermes* and *Illustrious*, three old battleships and four heavy cruisers in the region. The Japanese assumed that the Eastern Fleet was located in Colombo or Trincomalee, and perhaps both. Another two carriers and two battleships were believed to be headed to the region as reinforcements. With regards to the defences of Ceylon, these were assessed to be alert with surface patrols out to 200nm and air patrols out to 500nm. Nevertheless, it was anticipated that the Striking Force could achieve a surprise attack against bases on Ceylon because the Japanese believed that the Allies were oblivious to the coming Japanese attack.

Tone in May 1942 before departing for the Midway operation. This view shows the layout of the ship which cleared the entire aft portion of the ship for aviation facilities. In this May view, it carries one old Dave floatplane and three of the much more capable Jake floatplanes. In April, it carried only a single Jake. (Yamato Museum)

This is a Val taking off from *Akagi* during Operation C. The Val demonstrated its prowess as a ship-killer during the battle by sinking a total of nine Allied ships, including one carrier and two heavy cruisers. (Imperial Japanese Navy, now in the Public Domain)

On 19 March, the Striking Force issued its orders for the operation. Nagumo and his staff assessed that the British Fleet in the Indian Ocean consisted of three battleships, two carriers, four heavy and about 11 light cruisers. A considerable part of these forces was operating in the area of Ceylon and another part in the Bay of Bengal. Allied air power was assessed to be 500 aircraft in all of India, including Ceylon.

Leaving Staring Bay on 26 March, the Striking Force was ordered to transit south of Java and conduct a replenishment on 31 March. Depending on available intelligence on the British fleet, the Striking Force would advance to one of three positions south and east of Ceylon to conduct strikes against Colombo or Trincomalee as required. If no information on the British fleet was available by 4 April, the air strike would be pushed back a day to enable cruisers *Tone* and *Chikuma* to conduct a covert seaplane reconnaissance of Colombo or Trincomalee.

When attacking naval targets in Colombo or Trincomalee, each carrier would contribute nine fighters to gain air control over the target. The carrier attack bombers would carry bombs instead of torpedoes and have the target priority of aircraft carriers, battleships and then cruisers. The dive-bombers with their smaller bombs had the priority of carriers, cruisers, battleships and finally smaller ships, with some aircraft dedicated to attacking the airfield hangars. If the British fleet was determined to be split between Colombo and Trincomalee, the attack force would be split and both ports attacked simultaneously.

With 5 April set as the day of the air strikes on British facilities on Ceylon, Ozawa began to plan the operations of the Malaya Unit accordingly. His orders were issued on 17 March. The Malaya Unit was tasked to disrupt British SLOCs in the Bay of Bengal and to find and destroy British naval units operating in the area.

On 2 April, Ozawa would lead the Malaya Unit with light carrier *Ryujo*, five heavy cruisers, one light cruiser and four destroyers from the port of Mergui in southern Burma and advance into the Bay of Bengal. The transit route would follow north of the Andamans. Once in the Bay of Bengal the Malaya Unit Striking Force would break into three sections and be in position to attack shipping along the Indian coast by 4 April. The Centre

Unit, with the carrier, one heavy cruiser, one light cruiser and two destroyers was positioned between Madras and Calcutta. The Northern Unit with two heavy cruisers and a destroyer was placed in the waters south of Calcutta. The South Unit, also with two heavy cruisers and a destroyer, was positioned in the waters north of Madras. After ravaging shipping along the eastern coast of India, and after a series of small strikes from the aircraft from *Ryujo*, the Malaya Unit Striking Force was scheduled to reassemble on 6 April and transit back to Penang and Singapore by passing south of the Andamans.

Standing by near the Andaman Islands was the 11th Destroyer Division under the command of the 3rd Destroyer Squadron. This constituted the Guard Unit and was positioned west of the Andamans to guard the rear of the Malaya Unit. Also supporting the operation was a Supply Unit with an oiler escorted by two destroyers which was ordered to remain on standby in the waters near Port Blair.

Submarines were part of any large Combined Fleet operation, and in Operation C submarines were expected to play a major role. The commander of the 2nd Submarine Squadron, Rear Admiral Ichioka Hasashi, formed Submarine Unit C to provide direct support to the operation with six large submarines. In his orders dated 20 March, *I-7* was tasked to conduct air reconnaissance of Colombo and Trincomalee two days before the air attacks. *I-2* and *I-3* were stationed off the two ports to provide weather reports. The two boats of the 8th Submarine Division, *I-4* and *I-6*, were ordered to conduct searches for British naval units around the Maldive Islands and the Chagos Archipelago. After the air attacks, they were to be released to attack shipping, along with the late-arriving *I-5*.

The Striking Force departs Staring Bay on 26 March 1942. Ahead of *Zuikaku* are the four Kongo-class battleships. Operation C was the only time during the war that the four Kongo-class battleships operated together. (Imperial Japanese Navy, now in the Public Domain)

BRITISH

The fall of Singapore on 14 February 1942 marked the collapse of the British position in the Far East. Even before then, the Admiralty was working on the course of future operations with a draft document on 14 December titled 'Future British Naval Strategy'. It was approved by the service chiefs just days later. In it were the three principles that defined British strategy for the next six months which included the period of the Japanese thrust into the Indian Ocean. The strategy upheld the critical importance of the Indian Ocean and particularly of Ceylon which at that time was virtually undefended. It recognized that defence of the region was primarily a naval problem and that this burden would fall upon the RN without any American assistance. The third pillar of the strategy was the interdependence of the Indian Ocean and the Middle East. Both had to be protected concurrently.

Ceylon was considered the key by the British service chiefs. The loss of Ceylon risked the loss of India. This put access to Persian Gulf oil in great jeopardy; if the Persian Gulf oil was lost, the loss of the Middle East would follow since there were not enough tankers available to bring in oil from other sources. The British were even prepared to risk Calcutta and north-east India if it meant weakening the defences of Ceylon.

Maintaining control of Indian Ocean and Persian Gulf SLOCs required a strong Eastern Fleet. In spite of the RN's other commitments, it immediately began a dramatic reinforcement of the Indian Ocean. As described above, the fleet that was built to defend the Indian Ocean and Ceylon in particular was recognized to be inferior to a potential IJN force. The chiefs of staff considered that the best course of action for an inferior Eastern Fleet was to act as a 'fleet in being'. This would complicate any Japanese move into the region and force the Japanese to deploy major forces for any operation. The British believed that it was unlikely that the Japanese would make a major attack into the Indian Ocean since this would leave them exposed in the Pacific against the USN. While a major Japanese offensive in the region was ruled out, there was a point of view on the British planning staff that the IJN had a moment of opportunity to deploy a fleet superior to that of the British in the Indian Ocean before the USN was in a position to intervene. Once in the Indian Ocean, this superior Japanese fleet would search for an opportunity to destroy the Eastern Fleet; if this happened, all of India and Ceylon would be open to attack. If the Eastern Fleet declined battle, the Japanese would raid its bases in the region thus decreasing its ability to operate. In fact, this alternative view was what happened in April 1942.

Though Somerville was evidently well aware of the inferiority of the Eastern Fleet and the critical role it played in overall British strategy, there seems some doubt about his interpretation of his orders. On 11 March before leaving for Ceylon, Somerville told the First Sea Lord, Admiral of the Fleet Sir Dudley Pound, that the Eastern Fleet should operate as a fleet in being and not risk an engagement against a superior Japanese force. Loss of the Eastern Fleet meant potential disaster in the Indian Ocean. Pound saw the situation in the same way and expressed this view in a message for Somerville on 19 March. In this directive, Pound ordered Somerville to protect British SLOCs in the Indian Ocean but to do so using the Eastern Fleet as a fleet in being. He was not to take unnecessary risks or subject his fleet to heavy losses or attrition. The Admiralty identified the most likely

IJN courses of action as being coastal attacks in the Bay of Bengal and a Pearl Harbor-style surprise attack on Ceylon. These were clear orders and represented an accurate summary of Japanese intentions, but even so Somerville took incredible risks and ended up losing a sizeable portion of his fleet.

Having decided that the Japanese were coming with only two carriers, Somerville and his staff decided on an aggressive plan. This required a new set of assumptions. With the advice of the RAF, Somerville assessed that the Japanese carrier force would move to a point 100nm south-east of Ceylon for simultaneous strikes on Colombo and Trincomalee. The Japanese were expected to launch a moonlight strike and make a recovery at dawn.

This view of a strike preparing to take off from *Akagi* was taken during the Indian Ocean raid. The aircraft in the foreground are Zeros and those behind are Vals. Based on the number of aircraft visible (17 Vals and three Zeros), this photograph could have been taken on either 5 or 9 April as the aircraft prepared to launch against British naval units. (Imperial Japanese Navy, now in the Public Domain)

To detect the approaching Japanese, Somerville ordered his small Catalina force to conduct searches on the south-east sector of Ceylon out to 420nm. The Eastern Fleet was moved to Port T so as to be clear of the ports on Ceylon. The fleet would depart Port T on 30 March and move to a position south of Ceylon. From this location to the south-west of the expected Japanese advance, Somerville would be in position to ambush the enemy. This could be accomplished by staying out of range of Japanese day searches and then closing on the Japanese to execute a night torpedo attack.

This was a bad plan because it was based on a series of bad assumptions. The fact that the British assessment gravely underestimated the size of the Japanese carrier force and that they had assessed the wrong date for the air attack have already been discussed. On top of these major errors, there were others that made Somerville's plan not just worthless but dangerous. One was the assumption that the Japanese launch point would be to the south-east of Ceylon. The real Japanese approach route was from the south of Ceylon. Had the Japanese arrived off Ceylon as the British predicted on 30 March for a 1 April attack, they would have been to the south-west of the Eastern Fleet positioned between Somerville's fleet and Port T. For the tactical assumptions of the Japanese plan, it appears Somerville and his staff were guilty of a severe case of mirror imaging. The assumption that the Japanese would launch a simultaneous attack on two targets with only two carriers was totally misguided. The assumption that this would occur at night was based on how the British would conduct such an operation and not on recent Japanese carrier operations that the British were fully aware of.

The biggest flaw of Somerville's plan was the assumption he could pull off a night attack and not suffer grievous damage in return. The basic problem here was that the doctrinal search range of Japanese search aircraft was at least 300nm compared with the 100nm strike range of an Albacore. To execute a successful night attack, the Eastern Fleet would have to remain undetected during the day and make a high-speed dash towards the last known position of the Japanese carriers. Unless the location of Nagumo's fleet was known with a high degree of certainty, the ASV 2-equipped Albacores would have to search a large area for the Japanese. The radar aboard these aircraft had only an approximate 15nm range and the crews executing the search were inexperienced. If the Japanese were found, a strike would have to be executed at short notice. Then the Eastern Fleet would have to get beyond Japanese air search range by daylight. This entire endeavour left no margin for error.

THE CAMPAIGN

OPENING JAPANESE MOVES

The clearing of the waters around Singapore was completed on 24 February, and the Strait of Malacca was cleared on 5 March. Operation *T* kicked off on 8 March and was completed by 31 March. Operation *D* began on 20 March and was completed by 30 March. Meanwhile, the IJA continued its advance into Burma. Rangoon was captured on 8 March. To conduct the advance in central and northern Burma, the IJA planned to move the 56th and 18th Divisions by sea to Rangoon. This was a critical movement since movement over land would have taken considerably longer. Operation *U* began on 19 March and was completed by 28 April. During this period, 134 trips by transports were made. The operation was a complete success with only two empty IJA transports being lost to Allied submarines on the return trip from Rangoon to Singapore.

THE INVASION OF THE ANDAMAN ISLANDS

Departing from Penang on 10 March, the invasion force of the 2nd Battalion, 56th Infantry Regiment with the IJN's 12th Special Base Force was escorted by the Malaya Unit to its landing point on Ross Island in the Andamans. Cover was provided by the 22nd Air Flotilla operating from bases in Thailand, Malaya and northern Sumatra. The transit went without incident. The landing occurred during the early morning hours of 23 March. The British garrison of 23 officers and 300 Indian troops surrendered without offering resistance. The Japanese quickly established a seaplane base at Port Blair on 24 March and moved seven large flying boats there. These supported the subsequent raid into the Indian Ocean by flying daily search missions 600nm from the Andamans out to about 150nm from the Indian coast.

The invasion of Christmas Island was also successful. The Japanese coveted the island for its phosphate deposits and as the location of a possible airfield (the island turned out to be unsuitable for an airfield). The IJN assembled a large invasion force built around three light cruisers, the 4th Destroyer Squadron with eight destroyers, one oiler and 850 men of the 21st, 24th Special Base Forces and the 102nd Construction Unit carried aboard two transports and two converted destroyers.

This is *Naka* on 22 April 1942 entering Seletar Naval Base at Singapore for repairs after being torpedoed by USN submarine *Seawolf* on 31 March. *Naka* was the only Japanese ship to be damaged during the course of the Combined Fleet's extensive Indian Ocean operations during March and April. (Yamato Museum)

The landing was unopposed on 31 March with the small British-Indian garrison immediately surrendering. However, the American submarine *Seawolf* was stationed off the island and launched an attack against light cruiser *Naka*. A salvo of three or four torpedoes all missed and Japanese counter-attacks against the submarine were unsuccessful. The next morning *Seawolf* got another crack, this time at light cruiser *Natori* with three torpedoes. These also missed. The persistent *Seawolf* launched another attack that evening, this time at *Naka*. Of the two torpedoes fired, one hit the light cruiser near its No. 1 boiler. *Seawolf* survived ineffective Japanese counter-attacks. *Naka* also survived, being towed by *Natori* to safety at Bantam Bay on Java.

THE STRIKING FORCE ENTERS THE INDIAN OCEAN

The original timeline was for the Striking Force to depart Staring Bay on 21 March and attack Ceylon on 1 April. This was changed when the 5th Carrier Division was withheld in home waters to prevent an attack on the homeland by USN carriers. The new departure date was set for 26 March with an anticipated attack date of 5 April. The 5th Carrier Division arrived in Staring Bay on 24 March; two days later the Striking Force departed. The transit to Ceylon was uneventful. Daily reconnaissance and antisubmarine missions flown from the carriers revealed nothing.

On 3 April, the Striking Force refuelled. The following day, the Japanese maintained their steady course to the north-east, confident that on 5 April they would catch the Eastern Fleet in another Pearl Harbor-style attack.

As the Striking Force headed towards Ceylon, the Malaya Unit was also set in motion. Its first units arrived at Selatar Naval Base at Singapore on 27 February. Once all the ships had gathered, the entire force moved through the Malacca Strait to Mergui in the southern part of Burma.

On 26 March 1942, the Striking Force departed Staring Bay. In this dramatic photo taken from *Akagi*, the other major units of the fleet can be seen. In column behind *Akagi* are *Soryu*, *Hiryu*, *Hiei*, *Kirishima*, *Haruna*, *Kongo*, *Zuikaku* and *Shokaku*. Operation *C* was only the second time that at least five carriers of the Striking Force were committed to the same operation. (Imperial Japanese Navy, now in the Public Domain)

The first glitch with the Japanese plan involved pre-attack reconnaissance planned for the submarines. The submarine floatplane mission over Colombo was cancelled on 3 April. *I-7* had tried to approach the port on the previous two days and found British patrol activity south of the base to be heavy. Since it was required to surface to assemble and then launch the short-ranged floatplane, the reconnaissance mission was judged to be too dangerous by the boat's skipper. *I-2* attempted to close on Trincomalee on 4 April but also found that British patrol activity was heavy.

SOMERVILLE'S MANOEUVRING

From 30 March through 5 April, Somerville aggressively manoeuvred the Eastern Fleet to execute an ambush on what he believed was a Japanese carrier raiding force. This is a photo of *Formidable* steaming in formation with *Warspite* and an armed merchant cruiser. This photo was taken some time after the battle. (Royal Navy, now in the Public Domain)

Certain he knew the approach track of the Japanese and the date of their opening attack, Somerville departed Port T on 30 March and steamed to a position south of Ceylon. For the next two nights he advanced at night to the assessed Japanese launch position south-east of Ceylon. Of course, the British found nothing on either night. RAF searches from Ceylon also failed to find anything. As there was no sign of the Japanese, Somerville grew more concerned that operating in the same area for the last three days increased the chance that his fleet would be spotted by a Japanese submarine. Somerville feared the reason the Japanese had not made an appearance was that his fleet had been discovered and that the Japanese were simply waiting until the need to refuel forced him to return to Colombo or Trincomalee. After a final sweep with still no result, late on 2 April Somerville abandoned this plan and headed to Port T. He had little choice in the matter since the low endurance of the four R-class battleships demanded that they be refuelled.

After concluding that the intelligence was faulty and that there was no prospect of a Japanese air attack on Ceylon, Somerville detached several ships on 2 April to resume or begin their scheduled overhauls. Heavy cruisers *Cornwall* and *Dorsetshire* were sent to Colombo, and carrier *Hermes* with destroyer *Vampire* were sent to Trincomalee.

The Track of the Eastern Fleet, 31 March–3 April 1942

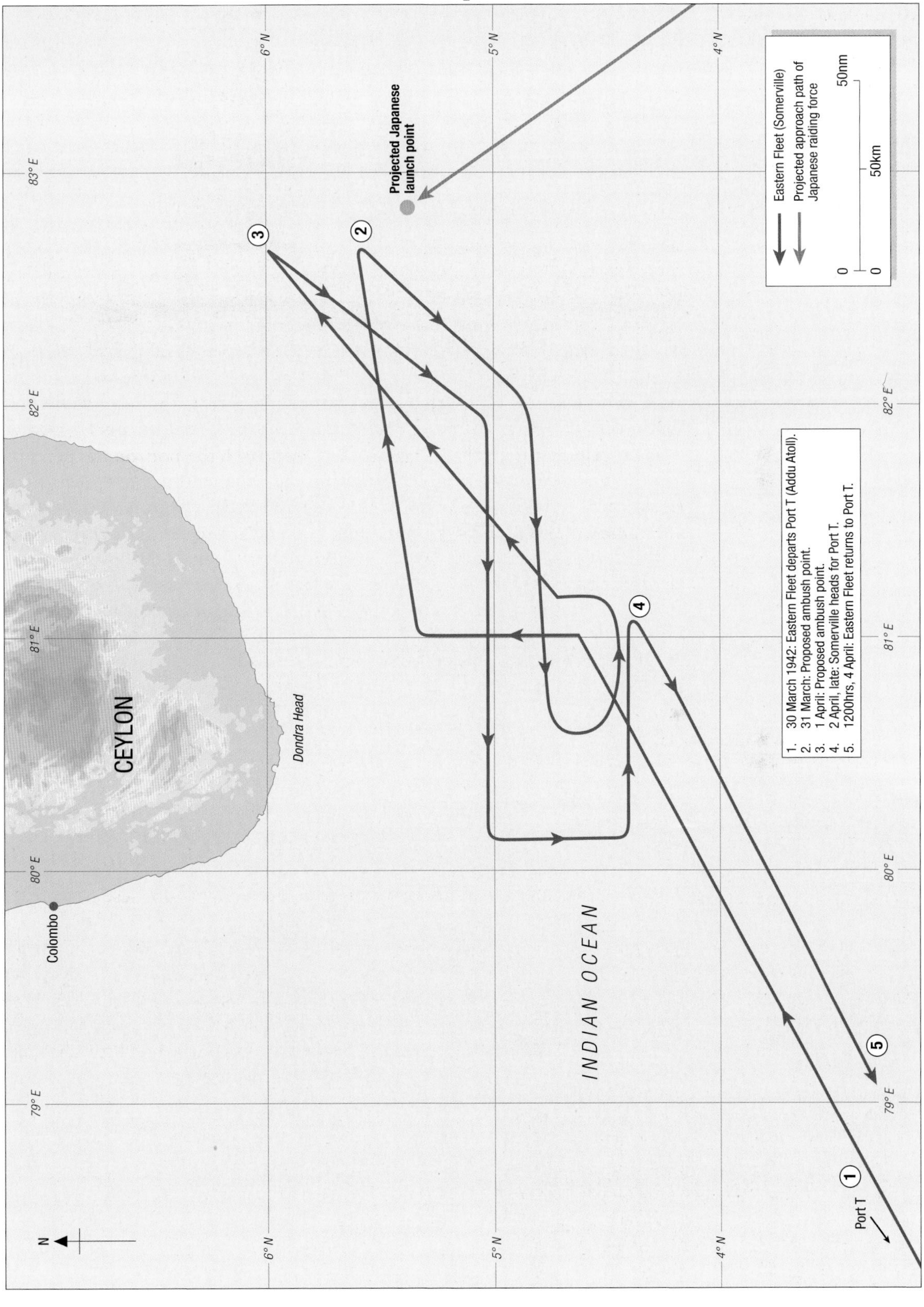

Projected Japanese launch point
Eastern Fleet (Somerville)
Projected approach path of Japanese raiding force
0 50nm
0 50km
1. 30 March 1942: Eastern Fleet departs Port T (Addu Atoll).
2. 31 March: Proposed ambush point.
3. 1 April: Proposed ambush point.
4. 2 April, late: Somerville heads for Port T.
5. 1200hrs, 4 April: Eastern Fleet returns to Port T.
CEYLON
Colombo
Dondra Head
INDIAN OCEAN
Port T
N
6° N
5° N
4° N
83° E
82° E
81° E
80° E
79° E

THE STRIKING FORCE IS DETECTED

Force A arrived at Port T at 1200hrs on 4 April. Force B followed three hours later. Their time in this very austere facility proved to be short.

Flying from their base at Koggala south of Colombo, the few operational Catalinas maintained a heavy schedule of long-range patrols. One of the Canadian aircraft had taken off at 0615hrs on the morning of 4 April to search the area south of Ceylon. Just before 1600hrs, the crew spotted a ship which turned out to be part of a large task force. The formation was 360nm from Dondra Head on southern Ceylon at a bearing of 155 degrees. At first, the crew thought that the large formation was the Eastern Fleet.

In fact, this was the first British sighting of the Striking Force. At 1555hrs, *Hiei* spotted a Catalina to the north and fired guns at it to alert other fleet units. The alert fighters were launched, three from each carrier except *Hiryu* which launched six. By 1620hrs, the Zeros had forced the flying boat into the water. Destroyer *Isokaze* approached the downed aircraft and took the crew prisoner. One man was lost when the aircraft sank. The treatment of the six survivors was extremely harsh.

The Japanese response was too slow to prevent the Catalina from sending a series of radio messages indicating that the Japanese fleet consisted of at least three battleships and one carrier. These messages were sent in the clear and were monitored by the Japanese. The Japanese also intercepted the relay of the contact report from several different British stations. However, the full report was not received by the British, so the full strength of the Striking Force remained unknown to them. The Japanese force was reported some 300nm south-east of Ceylon, making it about 60nm west of Nagumo's actual location. The most important thing was that the Striking Force had been detected and surprise lost. Given the location of the Striking Force, its

Royal Canadian Air Force Squadron Leader Leonard Birchall, the 'Saviour of Ceylon', aboard a Catalina aircraft before being shot down and captured south of Ceylon on 4 April. His discovery of the Striking Force ensured the Japanese attack was not a surprise. (Public Domain)

The small force of American-built Consolidated Catalina flying boats launched from Ceylon performed well during the battle. Despite the small number of operational aircraft, they detected the approach of the Striking Force before it attacked both Colombo and Trincomalee. (Library of Congress)

intentions were obvious. Despite being detected, Nagumo decided that the air raid on Colombo scheduled for the next day would proceed as planned.

When he heard about the Catalina sighting, Somerville's force had just arrived at Port T. He immediately prepared to depart as soon as refuelling was completed. This immediate decision to leave Port T and head towards the Japanese was criticized by Vice Admiral Willis and members of Somerville's staff. Though the full composition of the Japanese force was unknown, Somerville reverted to the original intelligence that the Japanese fleet was only a raiding force that he could use his night torpedo attack tactic against. It was wise for Somerville to leave Port T since he could not be sure that its existence was unknown to the Japanese, but a wiser course of action would have been to linger beyond Japanese search range until the true strength of Nagumo's force was known. Against the might of Nagumo's force, Somerville's rush to the east was a very risky gambit.

Unable to stop the Japanese from striking Colombo but determined to attack them as they withdrew, Somerville got Force A (except for cruisers *Emerald* and *Enterprise*) to sea at midnight with Force B following at 0700hrs on 5 April. Arbuthnot ordered *Cornwall* and *Dorsetshire* to leave Colombo and head south to join Force A on the afternoon of 5 April. He also ordered 25 of the 46 merchant ships out of Colombo with three escorts. They were directed not to return until 1400hrs on 5 April. On Ceylon, Layton knew that an attack on Colombo was coming on 5 April and that the Eastern Fleet was in no position to intervene. However, he assessed that a moonlight attack was likely so ordered the defences on alert from 0300hrs.

Needing more information on the approaching Japanese, another Catalina from 205 Squadron took off at 1745hrs. The aircraft spotted elements of the Striking Force several times (2237hrs, and 0045hrs and 0648hrs on 5 April) but at no time did the crew spot the entire Striking Force. The last report, after which the Catalina was shot down and the entire eight-man crew lost, indicated that the Japanese force included two battleships, two cruisers and several destroyers.

Track of the Striking Force, 3–12 April 1942

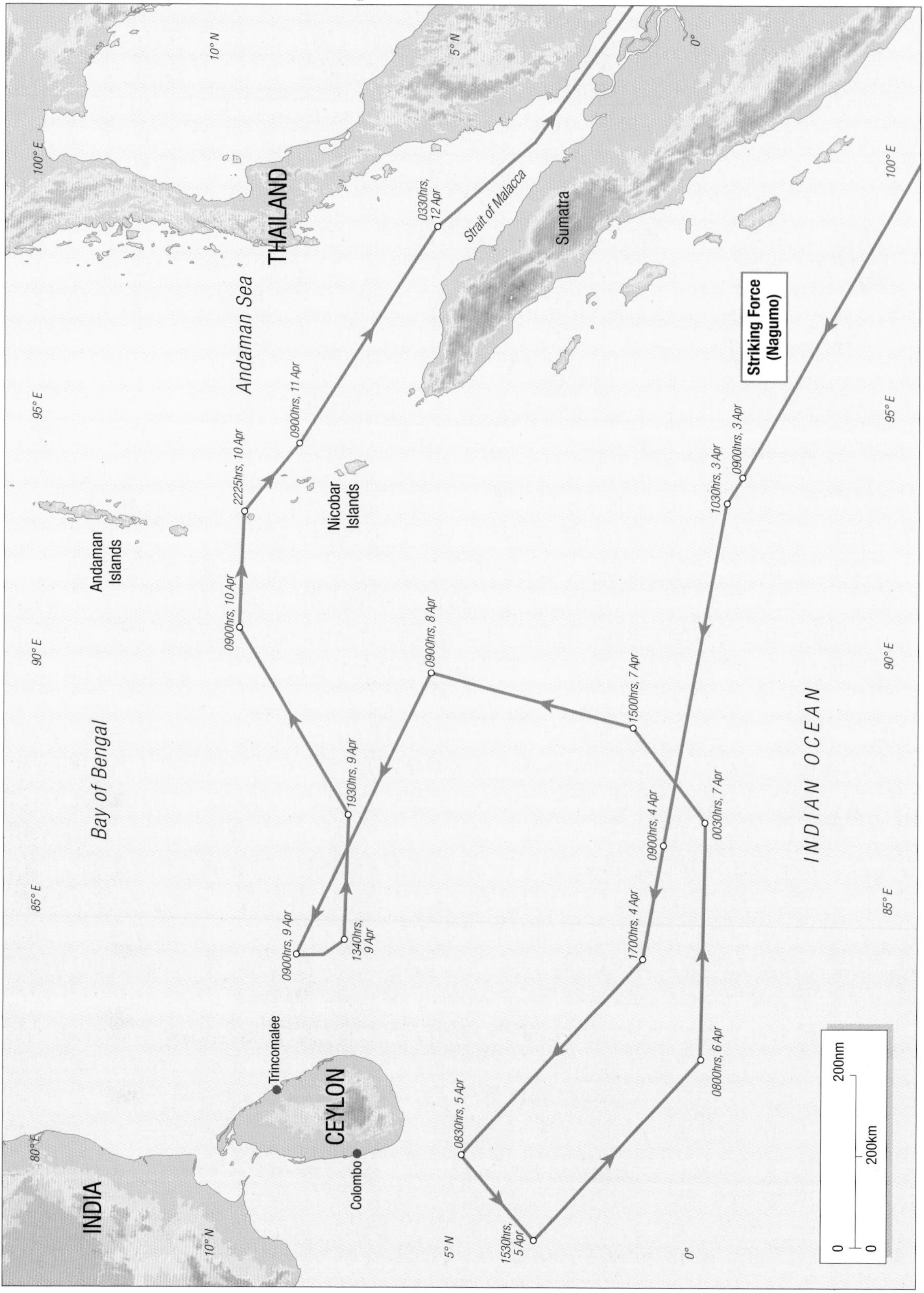

Map labels:
- 10° N
- 5° N
- 0°
- 100° E
- THAILAND
- Andaman Sea
- 0330hrs, 12 Apr
- Strait of Malacca
- Sumatra
- 0900hrs, 11 Apr
- 2225hrs, 10 Apr
- Nicobar Islands
- Andaman Islands
- 0900hrs, 10 Apr
- 95° E
- 0900hrs, 3 Apr
- 1030hrs, 3 Apr
- Striking Force (Nagumo)
- 90° E
- Bay of Bengal
- 0900hrs, 8 Apr
- 1930hrs, 9 Apr
- 1500hrs, 7 Apr
- INDIAN OCEAN
- 0900hrs, 4 Apr
- 0030hrs, 7 Apr
- 85° E
- 0900hrs, 9 Apr
- 1340hrs, 9 Apr
- 1700hrs, 4 Apr
- Trincomalee
- CEYLON
- Colombo
- 80° E
- INDIA
- 10° N
- 0830hrs, 5 Apr
- 0800hrs, 6 Apr
- 5° N
- 1530hrs, 5 Apr
- 0°
- 200nm
- 200km

42

THE ATTACK ON COLOMBO

As was the case at Pearl Harbor and Darwin, the Japanese planned to launch a massive first strike at Colombo. All five carriers contributed aircraft to the single wave attack by 127 aircraft. The strike was under the command of Commander Fuchida Mitsuo from *Akagi*.

Japanese Strike on Colombo, 5 April 1942

Unit	Aircraft	Carrier	Target
1st Attack Unit	17 Kate	*Akagi*	Ground facilities and ships
3rd Attack Unit	18 Kate	*Soryu*	Same
4th Attack Unit	18 Kate	*Hiryu*	Same
15th Attack Unit	19 Val	*Shokaku*	Ships and airfield by bombs and strafing
16th Attack Unit	19 Val	*Zuikaku*	Same
1st Air Control Unit	9 Zero	*Akagi*	Escort and strafing ground facilities
3rd Air Control Unit	9 Zero	*Soryu*	Same

The strike plan only committed 36 of the fleet's 90 fighters, so there were plenty available to provide CAP over the Striking Force. Each carrier launched only its dive-bomber or carrier attack bomber squadron leaving the other one in reserve. In this case, a second wave was not planned unless the harbour was full of naval targets that the first wave was incapable of handling. However, prudence dictated that a reserve be created to handle any naval targets that might be detected during the course of the first attack. This reserve was comprised of the dive-bomber squadrons aboard *Akagi*, *Soryu* and *Hiryu*. A total of 53 dive-bombers were readied for take-off on the three carriers and spotted on the flight deck for immediate launch. The carrier attack bombers on *Shokaku* and *Zuikaku* were fitted with torpedoes.

The standard Japanese carrier attack bomber of the period was the Kate. This is the Kate flown by Commander Fuchida off *Akagi*. The Kate was a versatile aircraft capable of performing as a level bomber and a torpedo-bomber; during Operation *C* it was only used as a level bomber. (Imperial Japanese Navy, now in the Public Domain)

Genda's original attack plan called for one massive strike with no aircraft in reserve. Given the early discovery of the Striking Force and the likelihood that many ships would leave Colombo before the morning attack, Nagumo decided to reduce the strike from 227 to 128 aircraft. This allowed for the creation of a large reserve to contend with any emergent naval targets. Only five aircraft were allocated to searches, all of which were floatplanes. Two Daves from battleships *Hiei* and *Kirishima* were given a route 180nm out from the Striking Force with a 30nm dog-leg before returning. Cruisers *Abukuma*, *Tone* and *Chikuma* all launched a single Alf on a route 250nm out with a 70nm dog-leg. The five aircraft covered the sectors south-west to north-west of the Striking Force. This was an inadequate number of search aircraft, and two of the aircraft were short ranged. It is hard to understand why this effort was so pathetic. It was probably the result of the pre-battle intelligence that indicated that a surprise attack would be achieved, but this convenient and inaccurate intelligence assessment should have been tempered by the fact that the Striking Force had been discovered the day before. Nagumo and his staff lacked the mental agility to adjust to this new reality.

Another indication that things were not going to plan for the Japanese was provided at 0645hrs on 5 April when one of *Hiryu*'s aircraft signalled that it had spotted a Catalina a few minutes earlier. The Catalina was shadowing the Striking Force by making skilful use of clouds. It was shot down at 0746hrs by *Hiryu* Zeros. This was the single Catalina from 205 Squadron which had survived the fall of Singapore. There were no survivors.

The Attack

Conditions at Colombo on the morning of 5 April, Easter Sunday, featured thunderclouds over the harbour and a low ceiling. Strike leader Fuchida gave the order to attack at 0745hrs. British radar had detected the approaching Japanese but the air warning network was incomplete so no warning was issued. The first sign that an attack was imminent was provided at 0740hrs when a large formation of aircraft was spotted to the south-west. There were already two Hurricanes from 30 Squadron and six Fulmars from 803 Squadron airborne. Despite the lack of warning, the British were able to get 41 more defending fighters in the air as their pilots were already in their cockpits when the Japanese were spotted. From Ratmalana Airfield came 20 Hurricane IIBs from 30 Squadron, and six Fulmars from 803 and 806 Squadrons. From the newly finished Racecourse, came 14 Hurricanes (nine IIBs and five Is) from 258 Squadron.

The Zeros under the command of Lieutenant-Commander Itaya Shigeru from *Akagi* led the Japanese assault. At 0732hrs the Zeros from *Hiryu* encountered six Swordfish from 788 Squadron near Colombo. The Swordfish were loaded with torpedoes and were on their way from China Bay to Ratmalana. It took only a few

Zero photographed aboard *Akagi* during Operation *C*. In spite of British efforts to enhance their air defences at Colombo and Trincomalee, escorting Zeros gained air superiority over both targets and inflicted heavy losses on defending British fighters. (Imperial Japanese Navy, now in the Public Domain)

minutes for the Zeros to shoot down all six of the lumbering biplanes.

The Zeros from *Soryu* were tasked to escort *Shokaku*'s dive-bombers. They bounced the six Fulmars on patrol over the harbour and quickly shot down two. The Hurricanes did not fare much better. The 21 fighters from 30 Squadron were never able to assemble into formation and were engaged by *Soryu* and *Akagi* Zeros and forced to fight a series of dogfights. This was playing to the strength of the Zero – 12 Hurricanes were shot down, with two crash-landing. The Japanese were able to establish some degree of air control over the harbour using 27 Zeros from *Soryu*, *Hiryu* and *Zuikaku*.

This is a 30 Squadron Hurricane IIB photographed at Ratmalana Airfield. Of the 22 aircraft in the squadron, eight were lost in combat against Zeros on 5 April. (Author's Collection)

Coming from the Racecourse, the 14 Hurricanes from 258 Squadron took off unmolested and were able to assemble before engaging a formation of dive-bombers. They shot down several dive-bombers before they were bounced by Zeros from *Hiryu*. Again, the Zeros made short work of the Hurricanes. Seven were shot down, and two more forced to crash-land. Of the five that returned to their base at 0835hrs, two were damaged. In the approximately 30-minute fight, the Japanese claimed that their fighters shot down 19 Spitfires, 21 Hurricanes, 10 Swordfish with torpedoes and one Defiant. Of these 51 aircraft, only nine were unconfirmed. This was an obvious exaggeration, but the reality was bad enough. Actual British losses were 27 aircraft – six Swordfish, four Fulmars and 17 Hurricanes; at least nine additional Hurricanes were damaged.

The Fairey Swordfish was the predecessor of the Albacore. It was also a capable torpedo-bomber but possessed a short range and was limited to night operations against modern fighters. (Naval History and Heritage Command)

Against heavy anti-aircraft fire and sporadic fighter attack, the 38 Japanese dive-bombers opened the attack on various targets around the harbour. The low ceiling of about 3,000ft affected bombing accuracy. The first to attack between 0750 and 0753hrs were Lieutenant-Commander Takahashi Kakuichi's dive-bombers from *Shokaku*. There were still plenty of targets in the harbour – Takahashi selected the largest one present, the 11,198-ton armed merchant cruiser *Hector*. At 0750hrs, he led his three-aircraft section into a dive and claimed a direct hit on the ship. Sixteen more dive-bombers followed; *Hector* was hit by four bombs and sank. The submarine depot ship *Lucia* was hit by a single bomb that created a large hole in the ship's hull. British anti-aircraft fire was reported to be heavy. In the middle of this attack, the dive-bombers were attacked by five Hurricane IIBs from 258 Squadron. One of the Japanese section leaders

A Hurricane IIB of 258 Squadron pictured on 5 April after its crash-landing after combat with Zeros on that same day. 258 Squadron lost nine of its 14 aircraft during the Japanese attack, of which two were forced to crash-land. (Author's Collection)

had his aircraft damaged and later crashed from fuel exhaustion on the way back to *Shokaku*.

The 19 dive-bombers from *Zuikaku* split their attack between shipping in the harbour and Ratmalana Airfield. Five selected the tanker *British Sergeant* for attack, but all their bombs missed. The other 14 headed for the airfield. Using the heavy clouds for cover, the Hurricanes and Fulmars bounced the approaching dive-bombers before they could deliver their weapons. Five were shot down. The surviving dive-bombers dropped their weapons on the airfield as the last four Hurricanes from 30 Squadron were taking off. One of the fighters was damaged by the blasts and had to abort its departure. During the dogfight, *Zuikaku*'s dive-bombers claimed six Hurricanes, but none were shot down. Overall results from the dive-bombers were disappointing for the Japanese. They claimed four large merchants, one small cargo ship and a tanker, as well as three hangars and a repair ship damaged. This was greatly exaggerated from the actual sinking of *Hector*, the damage to *Lucia* and minimal damage to the airfield.

Following the dive-bombers were the three squadrons of carrier attack bombers each carrying a 1,760lb bomb. The Kates from *Soryu* arrived over the target at 0756hrs, followed by those from *Hiryu* and *Akagi* in the next 12 minutes. Covered by Zeros from *Zuikaku*, they were largely unmolested by British fighters.

The 53 carrier attack bombers did their work between 0756hrs and 0813hrs. Dropping their bombs from high level, the B5N2s concentrated on the port area. Destroyer *Tenedos* was in refit and unable to depart; it suffered two hits and two near misses and sank with the loss of 33 men. Merchant ship *Benledi* was also hit, but the fires aboard were put out and the ship survived. Norwegian tanker *Soli* was also hit and was forced to beach. Damage to the workshops in the harbour area was extensive. Total casualties were 39 RN personnel killed and 49 civilians.

In view of the disappointing results of the attack and the many ships remaining in the harbour, at 0828hrs Fuchida radioed back to the Striking Force that a second strike was necessary. Fuchida's assessment was correct – the attack on Colombo had provided little benefit to the Japanese. The Zeros inflicted heavy losses on the defending British fighters, but the bombers were less impressive. Only two ships were sunk, both of little value, and three more damaged. Facilities at the naval base were heavily hit, but the port remained operational. Ratmalana Airfield remained operational, and the Racecourse was untouched. Japanese target selection for the Colombo attack was illogical. At Pearl Harbor, they ignored the naval base infrastructure; at Colombo, they focused on destroying this target category. This may have made sense if the Japanese long-term objective had been to prevent the Eastern Fleet from operating from this base. But the real Japanese goal was the destruction of British naval power, so the ships in the harbour should

The most numerous RN fighter, flying from carriers and land bases, was the Fairey Fulmar. It compared very unfavourably with the IJN's superb Zero fighter. This is an 803 Squadron Fulmar landing on *Formidable* at some point after the battle. (Royal Navy, now in the Public Domain)

have been the primary target. Of course, the Japanese assumption that they would achieve surprise in their Colombo attack and inflict a 'Pearl Harbor' on the Eastern Fleet was already thwarted, making the whole attack largely an exercise in futility.

For their part, the British were confident that they had inflicted considerable losses on the Japanese. After all the claims from 30 and 258 Squadron pilots were added to the Fulmar squadrons and the effects of anti-aircraft fire, 24 Japanese aircraft were confirmed lost, seven were claimed as probables and nine damaged. The actual tally was considerably less impressive. In addition to the one *Soryu* Zero lost in the air battle over the target, six dive-bombers were lost (five from *Zuikaku* and one from *Shokaku*) with another six damaged. No carrier attack planes were lost, but five were damaged.

Nagumo acted quickly on Fuchida's recommendation for a second strike. With no report from the search aircraft of any contacts, at 0852hrs he ordered that a second wave be created from the two squadrons of carrier attack bombers and the three squadrons of dive-bombers in reserve escorted by six fighters from each of the carriers. The order was given to take the torpedoes off the Kates and to replace them with 1,760lb bombs suitable for attacking land targets. A third of the dive-bombers on *Akagi*, *Hiryu* and *Soryu* were ordered to replace their 551lb semi-armour piercing bombs with 532lb high-explosive bombs.

At 0933hrs, Nagumo ordered Hara to launch aircraft to help guide back the returning strike. To accomplish this, at 0936hrs Hara launched six Kates (three from both of his carriers) with orders to form an east–west line some 5nm apart 50nm north of the Striking Force. Why Nagumo thought this additional assist was required to ensure the safe return of his strike is unclear, but the strike recovered safely between 0948hrs and 1025hrs. The six guide aircraft returned at 1250hrs.

Following the Japanese attack, the British attempted to strike back. Ten Blenheims from 11 Squadron, untouched by the attack on Ratmalana Airfield, were launched at 0830hrs and sent off in the direction of the Striking Force. They were unsuccessful since the location provided was incorrect.

Despite its age, having first entered service in 1937, the Kawanishi E7K2 Type 94 'Alf' possessed better capabilities than the more prevalent Dave floatplane. It was being replaced at the start of the war with the more modern Jake, and only three were available to the Striking Force in April 1942. (Naval History and History Command)

THE DEATH OF *CORNWALL* AND *DORSETSHIRE*

The strike on Colombo had garnered a disappointing haul; most disappointing of all was the absence of the British fleet. Nagumo's luck changed when at 1000hrs an Alf floatplane from *Tone* spotted what was described as 'Two enemy cruiser-like vessels' 150nm almost due west of the Striking Force. The search plane only spotted the cruisers as it was headed back to *Tone* on its return leg; the cruisers should have been found two hours earlier on the outbound leg of the search aircraft's pattern. The report was electrifying news for Nagumo and saved Colombo from a second attack. The fact that the ships were identified as cruisers was important. By doctrine, such heavily protected targets had to be attacked by torpedo-bombers since the relatively small bombs carried by dive-bombers might prove inadequate. To confirm the target identification and location, Nagumo ordered *Tone* and *Chikuma* each to launch their Jake floatplanes. At 1023hrs, he ordered the attack on the cruisers be conducted by the Kates from Hara's *Shokaku* and *Zuikaku* which required orders to stop the replacement of torpedoes with bombs and to remount the torpedoes. At 1030hrs, Nagumo quizzed Hara when his carrier attack bombers would launch with torpedoes. Hara replied at 1057hrs that the rearming operation would not allow a launch until 1300hrs. Nagumo did not like this answer so at 1118hrs ordered the strike to launch at 1200hrs and that any Kates that weren't ready at this time could follow when they had torpedoes.

In the middle of this exchange, the Alf from *Abukuma* reported at 1050hrs that it had spotted two destroyers 200nm to the west of the Striking Force. This prompted immediate doubts about the accuracy of the initial report from the *Tone* aircraft that British cruisers were present. Accordingly,

Nagumo altered his earlier command with a new order at 1127hrs that only the ready dive-bombers were to launch to attack the naval targets to the west. Between 1149hrs and 1203hrs, the 53 dive-bombers from *Akagi*, *Soryu* and *Hiryu* took to the air. Thirty-seven of the aircraft carried 551lb semi-armour piercing bombs but 16 carried 532lb high-explosive bombs suited for attacking land targets.

This frustrating situation for Nagumo was clarified when at 1155hrs the Jake floatplane issued a report that the two ships were cruisers. Still not believing the ship recognition skills of his aviators, *Tone*'s captain ordered the crew to confirm the types of ships. This was done at 1256hrs when the reply of the crew was received that indicated the ships were in fact Kent-class cruisers. This required Nagumo to once again order that the carrier attack bombers armed with torpedoes be included in the strike; Hara indicated that they would be launched at 1400hrs.

In fact, the Jake crew from *Tone* had made the correct identification. The two British ships were the heavy cruisers *Cornwall* and *Dorsetshire* which had departed Colombo at 2200hrs the night before and were headed south-west at high speed to rejoin Force A. Despite the fact that *Dorsetshire* carried radar, the British received no warning of the impending attack. At 1254hrs, the leader of the dive-bombers, Lieutenant-Commander Egusa Takashige, the IJN's most renowned dive-bomber pilot who had revolutionized Japanese dive-bombing tactics, radioed a report that he had spotted the two cruisers. Egusa manoeuvred towards the target so his aircraft would attack out of the sun and issued the order at 1329hrs to attack. What ensued between 1338hrs and 1355hrs was the most impressive display of dive-bombing by any nation during the entire war.

The Japanese claimed that 52 aircraft dropped their bombs – an incredible 46 hits were claimed. British reports assembled days after the event were incomplete, but they admitted that as many as 20 hits were scored with at least six more near misses being recorded. On this occasion, the Japanese claims of dive-bombing prowess were probably not much overstated. The British version of the action was incomplete and therefore unreliable. Egusa's airmen had put on an unparalleled display of dive-bombing. In perfect weather conditions, Japanese attacked in groups of three from dead ahead which blinded the defenders since this was out of the sun. The dive-bombers pressed their dive until 1,000ft altitude when they dropped their bombs. Egusa opened the attack by surprising *Cornwall*. Eighteen *Soryu* dive-bombers were followed by nine more from *Akagi*. The Japanese claimed 22 hits while the British were unable to do any better than to state the Japanese dropped 'about 18' bombs scoring ten hits, six near misses and two wide misses. Under this avalanche, *Cornwall* sank at 1355hrs.

The attack on *Dorsetshire* began only moments after the attack on *Cornwall*. The first three aircraft all achieved hits which knocked out half of its already inadequate anti-aircraft battery, destroyed its radios and knocked out steering. Once unable to manoeuvre, the cruiser was an easy target and many more hits followed – the Japanese claimed 24 hits from the 26 attacking aircraft (one

The destruction of British heavy cruisers *Cornwall* and *Dorsetshire* was the height of Operation *C* for the Striking Force. In only 17 minutes, both were struck by a large number of bombs and sunk. This Japanese photo shows the cruisers under attack and burning. (Imperial Japanese Navy, now in the Public Domain)

Cornwall was struck by as many as 22 hits over the span of a few minutes. Seventeen minutes after the assault began, it rolled over and sank. This is the cruiser just before it went under. (Imperial Japanese Navy, now in the Public Domain)

THE SINKING OF HEAVY CRUISERS *CORNWALL* AND *DORSETSHIRE*

Cornwall was attacked by 18 *Soryu* dive-bombers, followed by nine more from *Akagi*. The Japanese claimed 22 hits over the span of a few minutes; the cruiser rolled over, and sank at 1355hrs. The attack on *Dorsetshire* began shortly after the attack on *Cornwall*, knocking out its anti-aircraft capability and its steering. The cruiser was struck a total of 24 times, and sank only eight minutes after the first bomb was dropped.

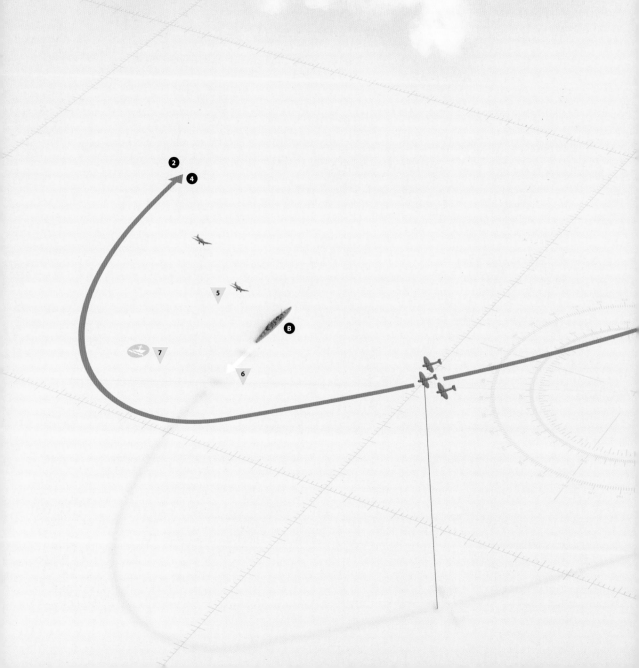

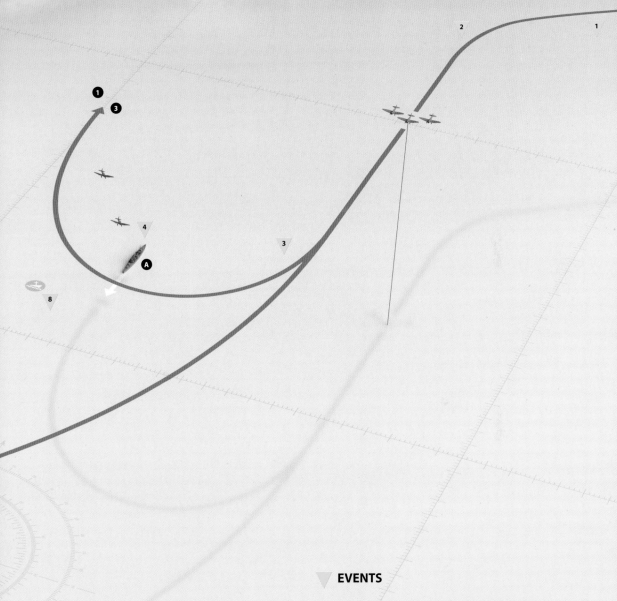

EVENTS

1. 53 Val dive-bombers approach the British ships from the north-east.

2. Egusa manoeuvres to attack the cruisers from ahead (downwind).

3. Egusa orders *Soryu*'s squadron to attack *Cornwall*, and *Hiryu*'s squadron to attack *Dorsetshire*; he splits *Akagi*'s squadron between *Cornwall* (nine aircraft) and *Dorsetshire* (eight aircraft).

4. 1338hrs: Egusa opens the attack and surprises *Cornwall*. The 18 *Soryu* dive-bombers claim 14 hits; the nine *Akagi* dive-bombers claim eight hits.

5. 1339hrs: Lieutenant-Commander Kobayashi Kakuichi leads *Hiryu*'s squadron to attack *Dorsetshire*. Of his 18 dive-bombers, 17 claim hits; the eight *Akagi* aircraft claim seven hits with one aircraft being unable to drop its bomb.

6. 1345hrs: *Dorsetshire*'s crew are ordered to abandon ship.

7. 1348hrs: *Dorsetshire* sinks.

8. 1355hrs: *Cornwall* sinks. Egusa reports: 'Two large cruisers sunk.'

BRITISH
A. *Cornwall*
B. *Dorsetshire*

JAPANESE
1. *Soryu* Carrier Bomber Unit (18 Vals)
2. *Hiryu* Carrier Bomber Unit (18 Vals)
3. *Akagi* Carrier Bomber Unit (9 Vals)
4. *Akagi* Carrier Bomber Unit (8 Vals)

Dorsetshire was subjected to as many as 24 bomb hits and sank after only nine minutes. By the time the crew was rescued the following day, 234 men had been lost. This is the cruiser just before it sank by the stern. (Naval History and History Command)

Akagi dive-bomber could not release its weapon). According to the official British account, the ship capsized and sank stern first only eight minutes after the first bomb was dropped.

The only good news for the RN in this debacle was that loss of life from the two cruisers was relatively low given the pounding they had received. The two crews totalled 1,546 men; survivors of the attack were forced to drift throughout the rest of the day and into the afternoon of 6 April in shark-infested waters. Somerville made it a priority to send ships to their rescue as soon as possible even though the Japanese were still thought to be in the area. On the late afternoon of 6 April, cruiser *Enterprise* and two destroyers arrived to pluck the men out of the water. Remarkably, 1,122 were saved. Nevertheless, 190 men from *Cornwall* were lost and 234 from *Dorsetshire*.

The quick demise of the cruisers made the launch of the carrier attack bombers armed with torpedoes unnecessary. *Tone*'s Jake reported no other contacts in the area, even after heading another 50nm to the south-west along the projected track of the two cruisers. Had the floatplane continued for another few miles, it would have spotted Force A which was only some 84nm from the location of the two sunken cruisers. Egusa's dive-bombers all returned by 1445hrs without the loss of a single aircraft.

SHADOW BOXING BETWEEN 5 AND 9 APRIL

The Japanese air attack on Colombo was clearly not the work of just two carriers. The actual raid consisted of 127 aircraft, and early British reports indicated that 75 aircraft were involved. Either way, Somerville should have examined his assessment that only two Japanese carriers were active in the region. Despite this new information, Force A was steaming at 18 knots towards the Striking Force. Force B was some seven hours behind. This brought the Eastern Fleet very close to peril. Force A was close enough to detect the Japanese air raid that sank *Cornwall* and *Dorsetshire* at 1344hrs 84nm to the north-east of *Warspite*. Somerville himself saw the radar return of the aircraft and identified it as a Japanese raid. Perhaps the British edge in radar underpinned Somerville's rash move directly for the Japanese carriers. If radar could detect and send fighters to destroy Japanese search aircraft Somerville probably believed he could remain undetected.

The battle that never was between the Eastern Fleet and the Striking Force came closest to happening on 5 April. Somerville assessed that the Japanese were lingering some 120nm south of Ceylon to recover aircraft. The actual track of Nagumo's force during this time was on an approach course of 315 degrees, followed by a turn to the south-west (course 230 degrees) at 0830hrs, and after proceeding for about 100nm, a turn at about 1530hrs to course 135 degrees to retire from the area.

Tracks of the Eastern Fleet and Striking Force, 5–6 April 1942

N

CEYLON

Dondra Head

80° E

Colombo

0830hrs, 5 Apr

5° N

0°

80° E

INDIAN OCEAN

1530hrs, 5 Apr

1726hrs, 5 Apr

1400hrs, 5 Apr

75° E

Maldive Islands

75° E

0°

Port T

① ② ③ ④ ⑤ ⑥ ⑦ ⑧ ⑨

Eastern Fleet (Somerville)
Cornwall and *Dorsetshire*
Striking Force (Nagumo)

0   100nm
0   100km

1.   1600hrs 4 April: Reported position of Catalina sighting.
2.   0000hrs 5 April: Force A departs Port T.
3.   0600hrs 5 April: Colombo strike launched.
4.   0700hrs 5 April: Force B departs Port T.
5.   1346–1355hrs 5 April: *Cornwall* and *Dorsetshire* sunk.
6.   1400hrs 5 April: Albacore search launched.
7.   1600hrs 5 April: Albacores spot Striking Force.
8.   6 April: Striking Force departs the area.
9.   1110hrs 8 April: Eastern Fleet returns to Port T.

53

During the period from 0830hrs until 1530hrs when Nagumo was headed to the south-west, Somerville had the Eastern Fleet in a nearly reciprocal course as it headed to the north-east after departing Port T. At their closest point of approach when the British fleet turned away from the Japanese at 1726hrs, the two fleets were roughly 100nm distant.

As already detailed, the Japanese launched their strike on the two British cruisers at 1145hrs. The *Tone* search aircraft sent to confirm the identity of the British ships continued to search some 50nm down the projected track of the doomed cruisers. It found nothing, but if it had continued to fly just a few additional minutes, it could have spotted Force A. Once Nagumo recovered his dive-bombers after their destruction of the two British cruisers, he ordered a course change to the south-east to clear the area. Even after sinking the two cruisers which he thought could be part of a carrier force, Nagumo made no attempt to launch a new search. This lackadaisical attitude towards conducting searches cost him the opportunity to locate the Eastern Fleet and strike it immediately with the two squadrons of armed torpedo-bombers not used against the cruisers.

The chances of Somerville mounting a night torpedo attack on the Japanese were dramatically improved by Nagumo's anaemic search efforts. At 1400hrs, the British launched four Albacores to search the 025–065 degree sector from Force A out to 200nm. The Striking Force was in the middle of this British search area. In fact, the two northerly Albacores made contact at 1600hrs. One issued a report that was slightly off in location and included no course, speed or enemy force composition. This Albacore was attacked by a Zero from *Hiryu*, but the British aircraft survived. The second Albacore failed to make a report and was shot down by a *Hiryu* Zero at 1628hrs. The presence of these carrier aircraft some 350nm miles from Ceylon should have set off alarm bells for Nagumo and his staff. Obviously, at least one British carrier was operating within close proximity of the Striking Force. Though there were two hours of light remaining, Nagumo ordered no additional searches. The only concession Nagumo made to this new reality was to order an alert for the remainder of the night and to prepare for a search in the morning. This was bound to be fruitless since the Striking Fleet maintained its course to the south-east throughout the night, away from the British. Nagumo's refusal to grab the opportunity to engage a British carrier force with the full power of the Striking Force defies understanding.

Even after the power of the Japanese carrier force was revealed in the aftermath of the attack on Colombo, Somerville persisted in his efforts to launch a night torpedo attack against the Japanese. Against the odds of this being successful, Somerville almost had his chance to unleash his Albacore force on the night of 5 April. This is a photo of Albacores launching from *Formidable* after the battle. (Royal Navy, now in the Public Domain)

The contact report from the first Albacore was received by Somerville at 1655hrs. The slightly erroneous report placed the Japanese only 125nm from Force A. At 1700hrs, more information reached Somerville that finally gave him pause. This was an FECB report from 1400hrs that the Japanese were on course 230 at 24 knots. By the time this report was received, the Japanese were already headed to the south-east, but when Somerville received the signals intelligence (SIGINT) report it indicated that the Japanese were headed right towards him. This, and the delayed realization that the Japanese force was superior to his own, prompted him to turn away at 1726hrs to open the distance from the Japanese. At this point, the nearest Japanese force was about 100nm distant, and the main body of the Striking Force was about 120nm away. The Japanese were oblivious to the presence of Force A on its right flank. Had Somerville not decided to turn away and continued his course to the east, Nagumo's 2nd Carrier Division might have passed within 20nm of Force A at about 2100hrs.

This was the chance Somerville had taken so many risks for. Unfortunately for the British, he was unaware of the almost perfect position Force A was in to launch a night torpedo attack on the unsuspecting Japanese. Nagumo's vulnerability was increased by the fact that the Striking Force was divided with the 2nd Carrier Division still trailing behind the main body. Not only was a strike by the approximately 30 available Albacores possible, but so was a surface attack by the British who employed radar when the Japanese had none.

The first modern carrier assigned to the Eastern Fleet was *Indomitable*. This is the carrier photographed in November 1941. It had the capacity to carry four squadrons, but this gave it a total aircraft capacity less than any of the Japanese carriers involved in the Indian Ocean raid and the aircraft it did carry were inferior to their Japanese counterparts. (Public Domain)

If the night attack could be executed before 2200hrs, Somerville would have some eight hours of darkness to get as far away as possible from Nagumo's force. By steaming at 20 knots, the British could have been some 260nm distant from the Striking Force (the 100nm strike range combined with the additional 160nm gained over eight hours). Keep in mind that while the maximum Japanese search range in 1942 was 300–350nm, none of the Japanese searches during the battle exceeded 250nm.

To launch an attack, Somerville needed more intelligence on Japanese movements. He was even worried that the Japanese could be headed to attack Port T. The three surviving afternoon search aircraft had landed by 1745hrs and their crews were quickly debriefed. The result was two signals from *Indomitable* that seemed only to contradict each other and failed to provide Somerville with the clarity he needed to launch a focused follow-up scout mission to locate the Japanese preparatory to launching a full strike. The first search Albacore was launched at 1930hrs but was sent to scout the northern arc instead of the eastern arc where the Japanese were located. A second Albacore was launched at 2100hrs, but it also was ordered to look to the north-east. By 2200hrs, the 2nd Carrier Division had rejoined Nagumo's main body and was located about 180nm due east of Force A. This was beyond the arc of the new search and beyond effective strike range. With no reliable information on the location of the Japanese, the night torpedo strike was cancelled. Somerville had lost his chance to ambush the Japanese.

Not until 6 April did Somerville fully realize the danger he was in. At this point his main objective became the preservation of the Eastern Fleet. After having no luck finding the Japanese with his night searches, Force A and Force B joined at 0700hrs. Somerville ordered that the fleet head east. According to his chief of staff, this was done for two reasons. Instead of moving away from the Japanese to the west, Somerville decided that

The Eastern Fleet's second modern carrier was *Formidable*, pictured here after the Indian Ocean raid. It arrived in the Indian Ocean in March 1942 and embarked an inexperienced air group of only 36 aircraft. (Royal Navy, now in the Public Domain)

moving to the east presented the best way to avoid detection. Of course, it was unknown to the British that the Striking Force was already headed away from Ceylon and there was no chance it could spot the Eastern Fleet whether it moved east or west. The second reason was moving east brought the fleet closer to the scene of the sinking of the two cruisers. With 1,500 men on these ships, it was important to rescue any survivors as quickly as possible. In his 6 April letter to his wife, Somerville stated that he was forced to hide with his inferior force.

At 1300hrs he sent *Enterprise* and destroyers *Paladin* and *Panther* to save any survivors from *Cornwall* and *Dorsetshire* under the cover of aircraft from Force A. This was highly successful as 1,122 men were saved.

In Somerville's and Layton's minds, the Eastern Fleet was still in jeopardy. They could not understand Nagumo's lack of a killer instinct; of course they had no idea that the Striking Force was headed away from Ceylon and the Eastern Fleet and that the Japanese had no intention of conducting an extensive search to detect the Eastern Fleet. Nevertheless, Layton was so concerned he sent a message to the Admiralty that the Japanese fleet was now assessed to include at least four carriers and three battleships and that it was operating somewhere between Port T and Colombo. The Eastern Fleet, Layton stated, 'now faces immediate annihilation'. This was intended as a warning to Somerville as much as it was issued as an update to London. The message was received on *Warspite* about 1400hrs and probably served to reinforce to Somerville the necessity of extracting the Eastern Fleet from danger.

By this point, Somerville had enough information to conclude that the Japanese force was comprised of four carriers and three battleships. This was a superior force to the Eastern Fleet and finally forced him into a very cautious mindset for the remainder of the battle. Another factor inducing caution was the decline in Force A's fighter strength to 25 operational fighters – six Martlets, eight Fulmars and 11 Hurricanes.

Somerville was sufficiently wary of the location of the Striking Force to decide to delay his return to Port T until the morning of 7 April. After completing the rescue operation, the fleet headed to the north-west while aircraft from Force A conducted searches out to 200nm. This plan was changed when one of the radar-equipped Albacores detected what were identified as two Japanese submarines to the south of the fleet at 0430hrs on 7 April. Somerville suspected that these were part of a submarine patrol line to the east of Port T. To avoid detection, he decided to change course to the north and approach Addu Atoll from the west by way of the Veimandu Channel. Only after a morning search on 8 April out to 175nm did Somerville feel safe enough to enter Port T at 1100hrs.

The Admiralty's concern over the safety of the Eastern Fleet only grew after the events of 5 April. It saw the inclusion of the four Royal Sovereign-class battleships in Somerville's force as nothing but an impediment. Accordingly, the Admiralty gave Somerville full discretion whether to keep them with his force or not. Since the attacks on Colombo and Trincomalee, both offered inadequate protection, and Port T none, the only alternative

This is *Abukuma* on 7 December 1941 as it was escorting the Striking Force in the Pearl Harbor operation. Japanese light cruisers were designed as destroyer squadron flagships. Dating from the 1920s, they had comparable capabilities to the RN light cruisers present in the Indian Ocean in April 1942. Note the presence of a floatplane on the aft catapult. (Yamato Museum)

was to withdraw the battleships to East Africa. After discussing this with his principal commanders, Somerville decided to send them to safety at Kilindini in Kenya. Once out of the reach of the Japanese, they could resume training and provide security to SLOCs in the region. Accordingly, Vice Admiral Willis departed Port T for Kilindini at 0200hrs on 9 April.

The realization that the Japanese force loose in the Indian Ocean was not a raiding force made Somerville examine how to ensure the safety of Force A. Clearly outclassed by the Japanese, he decided to keep it out of harm's way. Somerville decided to keep his force in Indian waters as a deterrent to the Japanese using light forces to attack SLOCs in the region. The Admiralty concurred but instructed him to keep out of bases on Ceylon and to use Bombay as his principal base. Four hours after Force B departed Port T, Force A also departed, this time for Bombay on the western coast of India. The RN's retreat from the eastern Indian Ocean was complete.

The redeployment of the Eastern Fleet was unknown to Nagumo. After a very hectic 5 April, the Striking Force launched a more concerted search on the morning of 6 April for the British carrier thought to be in the area. Instead of the anaemic search of 5 April with only five floatplanes, this time Nagumo assigned ten Kates to search the 180 degrees to the west of the Striking Force separated by 20 degrees between aircraft. Four floatplanes were assigned to search to the north-east and east. Of course, at this point there was no chance of spotting the Eastern Fleet which was far to the west. Had this type of search been made the previous day, Somerville's force would almost certainly have been spotted. On the 6th, the morning search failed to make contact, so Nagumo continued his track to the south-east and then shaped a course to the east to stay at least 450nm from Ceylon. The objective of this grand sweep around the east of Ceylon was to get into position to launch a strike against Trincomalee on the morning of 9 April. With any luck, this diversion out of the range of British searches and the delay from the 5 April attack on Colombo would lead the British to assess that the Striking Force had departed the region leading to some portion of the Eastern Fleet returning to Trincomalee. This was a naive idea to say the least, and again reflected Nagumo's inflexibility.

On 6 April, an aircraft from *Hiryu* on a search mission spotted a flying boat 70nm almost due north of the Striking Force. No contact was made at all on the 7th, but on the 8th *Abukuma* spotted a flying boat at 1520hrs. It opened fire but lost the contact at 1535hrs. Zeros were sent to make an interception, but the Catalina escaped into a squall. This was a Catalina from 240 Squadron and it had detected the Striking Force some 470nm south-east of Trincomalee and sent a contact report of three battleships and one carrier. This report was intercepted by the Japanese and this fact was sent to Nagumo aboard *Akagi*. This single Catalina was the only British search aircraft active on 8 April. Even though he knew he had been located, Nagumo decided to adhere to the 9 April attack on Trincomalee.

THE ATTACK ON TRINCOMALEE

Of course, the prime objective of the Japanese attack on Trincomalee was already on its way to Bombay and East Africa. When Arbuthnot learned of the Catalina's detection of the Striking Force on the afternoon of 8 April, he ordered 12 ships to depart Trincomalee. All but one was ordered to steam south within close distance of the coast of Ceylon and to be at least 40nm away from the port by dawn. The most important ships moving south were *Hermes* and destroyer *Vampire*; however, a corvette, a minelayer, three tankers and four other naval auxiliaries also departed. By the morning of 9 April, there were only two major warships in the harbour. These included the old Dutch cruiser *Sumatra* and the more valuable monitor *Erebus* which had a modern radar and six 3in anti-aircraft guns and had been sent to Trincomalee to provide a measure of air defence. In addition, there were nine freighters of 3,000 tons or more and eight small warships and naval auxiliaries still in the harbour.

For the sixth time in the war, the Striking Force prepared to deliver a hammer blow against an Allied target. Genda put together an attack plan outlined below:

Japanese Strike on Trincomalee, 9 April 1942

Unit	Aircraft	Carrier	Target
1st Attack Unit	18 Kate	*Akagi*	Naval arsenal and vicinity
3rd Attack Unit	18 Kate	*Soryu*	Same
4th Attack Unit	18 Kate	*Hiryu*	Headquarters of the Ceylon commander, barracks and anti-aircraft positions
5th Attack Unit	19 Kate	*Shokaku*	Airfield and seaplane base
6th Attack Unit	18 Kate	*Zuikaku*	Residences of naval commander and governor, barracks
1st Air Control Unit	6 Zero	*Akagi*	Escort
3rd Air Control Unit	6 Zero	*Soryu*	Gain air control and strafe seaplane base
4th Air Control Unit	6 Zero	*Hiryu*	Same
5th Air Control Unit	10 Zero	*Shokaku*	Gain air control and strafe airfield
6th Air Control Unit	10 Zero	*Zuikaku*	Same

The best reconnaissance floatplane operated by the IJN in April 1942 was the Aichi E13A Type 0 'Jake'. However, only two were available to the Striking Force in April 1942. (Public Domain)

Fresh from the episode on 5 April when a British naval force was spotted near the Striking Force as the main Japanese strike was in the air, Nagumo held back a strong reserve to deal with emergent targets. The dive-bomber squadrons from all five carriers were kept in reserve (with a total of 85 aircraft) and a potential escort of nine Zeros, three each from *Akagi*, *Soryu* and *Hiryu*.

The events of 9 April unfolded eerily like those of 5 April. A Jake reconnaissance floatplane was launched from *Tone* at 0345hrs to conduct a covert weather reconnaissance over Trincomalee. This was detected by a British radar just to the north of Trincomalee. The strike of 91 carrier attack bombers armed with bombs and 38 Zeros began launching at 0600hrs. The morning CAP was also sent up, as were six more floatplanes from the battleships and cruisers to conduct search missions. Again, the number of aircraft was inadequate for a full search.

The few remaining Catalinas continued to do outstanding work. An aircraft from 205 Squadron took off from Koggala at 0526hrs and at 0708hrs spotted the Striking Force just over 200nm due east of Trincomalee. The Catalina was spotted and quickly engaged by fighters from *Hiryu*. It was shot down with no survivors. However, it was able to send a message before being shot down. Based on this report, the British sent up all available Blenheims from 11 Squadron to attack the Japanese fleet.

The Japanese force, arranged in three waves, was detected on radar at 0706hrs some 90nm to the east of Trincomalee. This was converted into visual contact at 0720hrs on the Japanese formation approaching at 15,000ft. Given the radar warning, the alert was sounded at China Bay Airfield about 4.5 miles south-west of the port. The British had time to get 16 Hurricanes airborne. Fuchida, again in command of the strike, had given the attack order at 0720hrs.

When the approaching Japanese were detected on radar, three Hurricanes were already aloft from 261 Squadron. These were vectored out to make an interception. They made visual contact 30nm from the coast and identified the bombers in two formations at 15,000ft, with the covering Zeros above at 21,000ft. The Hurricanes went to 22,000ft to gain a height advantage and conducted a diving attack from astern of the Zeros. Two of the Japanese fighters were flamed in the first pass; in the ensuing melee, one of the Hurricanes also went down.

AIR BATTLE OVER TRINCOMALEE (PP. 60–61)

In the second massive Japanese raid of the battle, on 9 April a total of 91 carrier attack bombers escorted by 38 Zero fighters were committed to shatter shipping and facilities at Trincomalee. On this occasion, the defending British were able to draw first blood.

At dawn, a patrol of three Hurricanes from 261 Squadron took off from China Bay Airfield and orbited at 15,000ft. When the radar at Elizabeth Point detected the incoming Japanese raid at 0706hrs, the Hurricanes were vectored out for an interception. Only minutes later, at 0715hrs, the British sighted the Japanese formation 30nm off the coast. According to the section leader of the Hurricanes, Flight Lieutenant David Fulford, the Japanese were at 15,000ft flying due west towards Trincomalee. The first group of Japanese aircraft was comprised of two 'V's of Kates from *Soryu* escorted by three Zeros from *Zuikaku*. Fulford ordered his section to turn north and gain altitude. Once the Hurricanes reached 22,000ft, they turned west to get behind the Japanese. The three Zeros were weaving behind the bombers. Fulford ordered each Hurricane to select one Zero for attack.

This battlescene shows the three 261 Squadron Hurricanes (**1**) diving to attack the Zeros (**2**). One Zero has already been hit and is burning (**3**). Below the fighter escort can be seen the two 'V's of Kates from *Soryu* (**4**). The attack resulted in two of the *Zuikaku* fighters being shot down. One of the Hurricanes was also lost in the ensuing dogfight.

Between 0710hrs and 0715hrs, another 12 Hurricanes were scrambled. Some of these were able to engage the Japanese bombers before the escorting Zeros intervened. The first group of Kates from *Soryu* arrived over the port area at 0730hrs. Three of these were damaged by Hurricanes. The second group from *Hiryu* was also attacked by Hurricanes with one Kate going down. The next two groups from *Akagi* and *Zuikaku* encountered no air opposition. The final group from *Shokaku* was heavily attacked

by Hurricanes; seven bombers were damaged. In all, the Hurricane pilots claimed four Zeros and four bombers and another three Zeros and another bomber as probable kills. In fact, only three Zeros and two Kates were lost. All of the Japanese losses were likely caused by the defending Hurricanes – though anti-aircraft fire was described as heavy, no Japanese aircraft were confirmed as lost to ground fire. However, it is possible that British anti-aircraft fire did have some success as one Zero was claimed by a 40mm Bofors unit and one Kate by a 3.7in anti-aircraft gun unit.

The claims by the Zero pilots were outlandish, a total of 54 British fighters. Actual British losses from the 16 Hurricanes that managed to get airborne were eight Hurricanes shot down or forced to crash-land, with another three damaged. The Fulmars from 273 Squadron failed to scramble. One Fulmar was lost in a morning reconnaissance flight and six were scrambled later in the day to defend *Hermes*.

Eighteen Kates with 1,760lb bombs went after the ships in the harbour. They flew in groups of six with the entire group dropping their bombs together following the lead aircraft. Dropping from an altitude of 9,000–10,000ft, their accuracy was not outstanding. Monitor *Erebus*, mistaken for a Leander-class cruiser, was a target but was only damaged by near misses that killed nine and wounded 22. *Sumatra* was probably hit by a bomb that failed to explode – it was able to leave Trincomalee on 16 April and head to Bombay. Merchant *Sagaing*, with deck cargo of a Walrus seaplane and three Albacores, was hit and set on fire. The ship had to be beached so became a total loss.

A least 12 bombers went after China Bay Airfield. These wreaked considerable damage, destroying 13 aircraft under repair (seven Swordfish, four Fulmars and two Albacores) and damaging other facilities. Only three men were killed and six wounded. Overall, damage was not crippling and the airfield remained in operation. The bulk of the level bombers attacked the dockyard and the other land targets listed on the chart above. Some 30 bombs were dropped on the naval installation and another 24 at the Governor's residence, barracks and coastal defence guns. The later targets only made sense if the Japanese planned a subsequent invasion, which of course they did not. The bulk of the raid was a waste.

In return for the significant resources devoted to the attack, the Japanese achieved little. Only one ship was sunk and two low-value warships damaged. British aircraft losses were heavy, 27 aircraft if the Catalina destroyed that morning is included. Damage to the airfield and naval base was repaired using local resources. Total personnel casualties were 68 killed and 41 wounded.

Japanese losses were comparatively light: three Zeros and two carrier attack bombers (both from *Hiryu*). In addition, 11 Kates were damaged,

All five carriers of the Striking Force contributed their carrier attack bomber squadron, a total of 91 aircraft, to the attack on Trincomalee. Despite this level of effort, little damage was inflicted on the British. Only two Kates were lost in the raid; this view shows two of the bombers over the target after they dropped their bombs. (Imperial Japanese Navy, now in the Public Domain)

Haruna running trails after its extensive modernization in 1934. Kongo-class battleships were equipped with a catapult located between No. 3 and 4 14in turrets. Each could carry three floatplanes. One of Haruna's Dave floatplanes spotted carrier Hermes on the morning of 9 April. (Yamato Museum)

probably all by Hurricanes. Total Japanese aircrew casualties were eight killed and one wounded. The strike returned at 0930hrs.

On 9 April, Nagumo was slightly more attentive to search operations than he had been on 5 April. Six search floatplanes were launched before the Trincomalee strike took off. They were ordered to search the 180 degrees arc to the west of the Striking Force out to 150nm. This covered the waters between the Striking Force and Ceylon making it all but certain that the British ships fleeing Trincomalee would be spotted. The aircraft searching where Hermes was located was a Dave from battleship Haruna. Contact was made as the floatplane was making its last turn for the return trip back to its parent ship. The contact report was sent in the clear and intercepted by the British at 0858hrs. Within 30 minutes, a warning was sent to Hermes and RAF fighters were ordered to proceed to its location to provide air cover.

The report from Haruna's floatplane that it had spotted carrier Hermes and 'three destroyers' placed the British ships just 155nm west-south-west of the Striking Force. Within five minutes Nagumo ordered his alert aircraft to prepare to take off to deal with the threat. The short-ranged floatplane sent a final message and then headed back towards Haruna; it lacked the endurance to shadow Hermes. The launch of the strike force began at 0843hrs with 85 dive-bombers and nine escort fighters. This time the dive-bombers were led by Lieutenant-Commander Takahashi Kakuichi from Shokaku. After arriving at the anticipated location of Hermes at 0950hrs and finding nothing, Takahashi flew south for 40nm before reversing course and finally spotting Hermes at 1030hrs.

Takahashi ordered an immediate attack at 1035hrs. For the first time in history, carrier-borne aircraft attacked a carrier. For the second time in five days, the Japanese dive-bomber pilots displayed phenomenal skill. Over the next few hours, the 85 dive-bombers sank six ships, claiming 67 hits in the process.

Hermes and Vampire had departed Trincomalee at 0100hrs and were about 65nm south of the port and about 5nm off the coast when they were spotted by Haruna's floatplane. At 0900hrs, the small force had turned back to the north so as to return to Trincomalee as ordered by 1600hrs. Seven miles to the south-east was tanker (not Royal Fleet Auxiliary as is often stated)

Athelstane with corvette *Hollyhock*. To the north was the tanker *British Sergeant* which had also changed course to the north for a return to port.

When the Japanese spotted *Hermes*, the contact report was intercepted by the British. At 0953hrs, Arbuthnot ordered *Hermes* to make full speed to Trincomalee to get under the air umbrella of the fighters based there. The RAF tried to arrange air cover for the carrier but the Hurricanes from China Bay sent to defend the carrier were recalled to defend Trincomalee after an alert was issued that Japanese aircraft were sighted over the port. Only at 1100hrs did the first group of Fulmars depart Ratmalana at Colombo, followed by a group of six Fulmars from 273 Squadron based at Kokkilai at about 1120hrs. This was too late to defend the vulnerable ships trying to return to Trincomalee. Defence therefore rested on the anti-aircraft guns of the threatened ships but none of them were well equipped to deal with concerted air attacks. For example, *Hermes* carried three 4in guns, two quad machine guns and about six 20mm guns, whereas *Vampire* embarked a single 3in gun and a small number of lighter weapons.

With *Hermes* as the target, the Japanese onslaught began at 1040hrs with Takahashi leading *Shokaku*'s 18 dive-bombers against the carrier in perfect conditions for dive-bombing. Takahashi claimed a hit, as did 12 more of his fellow pilots. Next up were the 14 Vals from *Zuikaku*, which also claimed 13 hits. The pounding continued with 11 *Hiryu* aircraft making their attack (claiming nine hits) and two from *Akagi* (both claiming hits) before it was obvious the carrier was doomed. The Japanese claim of 37 hits from 45 bombs dropped seems incredible, but the senior surviving officer from *Hermes* stated that at least 40 bombs hit the ship. Within 15 minutes of the attack beginning, *Hermes* sank with the loss of 306 of 790 crewmen.

Hermes was helpless in the face of almost three full squadrons of Japanese dive-bombers. Late on the morning of 9 April, the carrier was attacked under perfect conditions for the Japanese, just off the coast of Ceylon. Of the 45 dive-bombers that selected *Hermes* as their target, 37 claimed hits. This was one of the few times in the war when Japanese aviators did not exaggerate their success. (Imperial Japanese Navy, now in the Public Domain)

THE JAPANESE DIVE-BOMBER ATTACKS ON 9 APRIL 1942

For the first time in history, carrier-borne aircraft attacked a carrier. The 85 Japanese dive-bomber pilots displayed phenomenal skill, sinking six ships: the carrier *Hermes*, the destroyer *Vampire*, the corvette *Hollyhock*, the tankers *Athelstane* and *British Sergeant*, and the freighter *Norviken*.

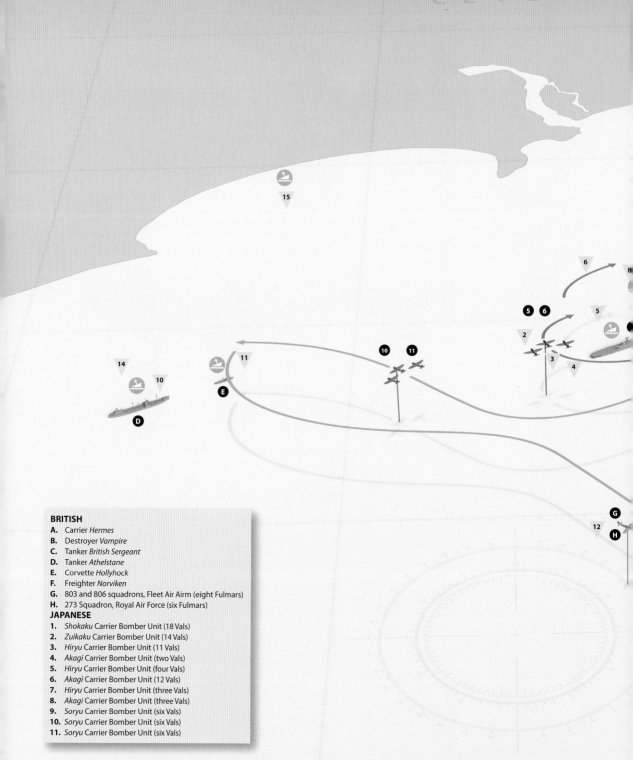

BRITISH
- **A.** Carrier *Hermes*
- **B.** Destroyer *Vampire*
- **C.** Tanker *British Sergeant*
- **D.** Tanker *Athelstane*
- **E.** Corvette *Hollyhock*
- **F.** Freighter *Norviken*
- **G.** 803 and 806 squadrons, Fleet Air Airm (eight Fulmars)
- **H.** 273 Squadron, Royal Air Force (six Fulmars)

JAPANESE
1. *Shokaku* Carrier Bomber Unit (18 Vals)
2. *Zuikaku* Carrier Bomber Unit (14 Vals)
3. *Hiryu* Carrier Bomber Unit (11 Vals)
4. *Akagi* Carrier Bomber Unit (two Vals)
5. *Hiryu* Carrier Bomber Unit (four Vals)
6. *Akagi* Carrier Bomber Unit (12 Vals)
7. *Hiryu* Carrier Bomber Unit (three Vals)
8. *Akagi* Carrier Bomber Unit (three Vals)
9. *Soryu* Carrier Bomber Unit (six Vals)
10. *Soryu* Carrier Bomber Unit (six Vals)
11. *Soryu* Carrier Bomber Unit (six Vals)

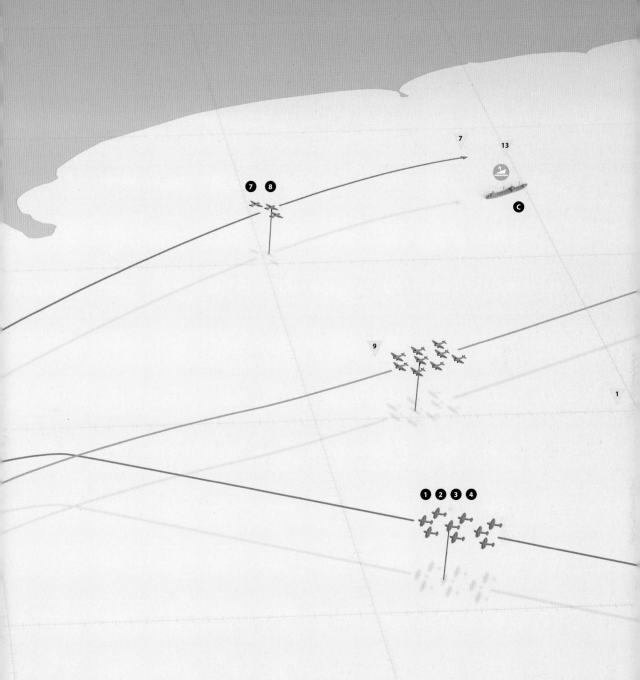

EVENTS

1. 1030hrs: Lieutenant-Commander Takahashi with 85 Val dive-bombers and an escort of nine Zeros spots *Hermes*; he orders the attack to begin at 1035hrs.

2. 1040hrs: Takahashi leads *Shokaku*'s dive-bomber squadron to attack *Hermes*.

3. 1045hrs: *Zuikaku*'s dive-bomber squadron attacks *Hermes*.

4. 1050hrs: 11 *Hiryu* dive-bombers attack *Hermes*, followed by two from *Akagi*.

5. 1055hrs: *Hermes* sinks having been hit by what the Japanese claim was 37 of 45 bombs aimed at it.

6. 1055hrs: *Vampire* attacked by four *Hiryu* dive-bombers and 12 from *Akagi*.

7. 1100hrs: *British Sergeant* attacked by three *Hiryu* and three *Akagi* dive-bombers.

8. 1102hrs: *Vampire* breaks in two, with the forward section sinking immediately and the aft section minutes later.

9. 1205hrs: After pursuing a false report of a second British carrier, *Soryu*'s dive-bomber squadron returns to attack three previously spotted ships.

10. 1205hrs: *Athelstane* and *Norviken* each attacked by six dive-bombers.

11. 1208–1218hrs: *Hollyhock* attacked by six dive-bombers. It sinks after two hits and two near misses.

12. *c.*1215hrs: Fulmars engage *Soryu*'s Carrier Bomber Unit; four Japanese aircraft are destroyed for the loss of two Fulmars.

13. 1300hrs: *British Sergeant* sinks.

14. 1430hrs: *Athelstane* sinks.

15. Early on 10 April: the abandoned *Norviken* runs aground.

DEATH OF A CARRIER (PP. 68–69)

The first time in naval history that carrier-based aircraft sank an enemy carrier was not in the Pacific during one of the carrier battles between the Americans and Japanese, but in the Indian Ocean between the British and Japanese. On the morning of 9 April, a Japanese search aircraft spotted *Hermes* south of Trincomalee with an escort of a single destroyer. Nagumo had five squadrons of Val dive-bombers standing by for just such an eventuality. Within two hours of spotting the British carrier, the Japanese dive-bombers began their attack.

The first to dive against *Hermes* were those from carrier *Shokaku* led by Lieutenant-Commander Takahashi. Conditions for the attack were excellent and *Hermes* was a relatively slow and ponderous target with limited anti-aircraft defences. What followed was an absolute master lesson in the art of dive-bombing. Of the 45 bombs dropped by the Japanese, they claimed 37 hits.

This was no exaggeration since the senior surviving British officer stated his ship was hit by at least 40 bombs.

In this scene, *Shokaku*'s Carrier Bomber Squadron is starting to execute its attack on the *Hermes* (**1**). Takahashi's Val (**2**) has completed his attack and another dive-bomber behind him (**3**) has just released its bomb. Of the 18 aircraft in the squadron, 13 claimed hits. *Hermes* fired back at the attackers with a mix of 4in and lighter anti-aircraft guns, but no Japanese aircraft were lost.

After *Shokaku*'s dive-bombers finished, dive-bombers from *Zuikaku*, *Hiryu* and *Akagi* piled on against the nearly defenceless carrier. Within 15 minutes, *Hermes* capsized to port and sank. From the crew, 302 were killed in the onslaught and four more died after being rescued. At least 139 were wounded, making for very heavy losses from a crew of about 790 men.

Tanker *British Sergeant* was unfortunate enough to be located near *Hermes* on the morning of 9 April. After the carrier was dispatched, six dive-bombers from *Hiryu* and *Akagi* used the tanker as a target of opportunity. According to its crew, the tanker was struck by four direct hits and two near misses and quickly sank. (Public Domain)

Even before *Hermes* had sunk, other dive-bombers went after *Vampire*. Four *Hiryu* dive-bombers claimed one hit and three misses, while all 12 of *Akagi*'s dive-bombers claimed to have hit their target. Within ten minutes the destroyer broke in half and went under. Despite this pounding, only nine of 119 crewmen were lost.

The nearby hospital ship *Vita*, on its way to Colombo, saw the attacks and stopped to pick up 595 survivors from *Hermes* and *Vampire* between 1300hrs and 1900hrs. Clearly marked as a hospital ship, it was not molested by the Japanese. Other men were saved by local craft or swam to shore unassisted.

As the *Hermes* and *Vampire* were being deluged by bombs, six dive-bombers attacked *British Sergeant* about 12nm to the north-west of *Hermes*. Six aircraft (three from *Hiryu* and three from *Akagi*) bombed the ship at 1100hrs. British sources state four direct hits and two near misses struck the ship, matching Japanese claims. The crew abandoned ship and the ship sank at 1300hrs.

The last dive-bomber squadron to attack came from *Soryu* led by Egusa. His squadron had taken off later than the rest of the strike. Upon reaching the target area, Egusa went searching to the north for a second carrier reported by *Abukuma*'s floatplane. After failing to find the non-existent carrier, Egusa decided to attack some ships he had spotted earlier. Tanker *Athelstane* and corvette *Hollyhock* were attacked south of *Hermes*' last position. *Soryu*'s aircraft also lined up for an attack on the small Norwegian freighter *Norviken*. Japanese sources state that each ship was attacked by six dive-bombers, but Allied sources differ. The British state that seven attacked *Athelstane* with their usual accuracy of five hits and two near misses. The crew abandoned ship and the tanker sank over three hours later.

Hollyhock was a Flower-class corvette launched in 1940. Built as an anti-submarine ship, it was totally unsuited to defend against air attack and carried only a single Mk VIII 2-pdr anti-aircraft gun. After two near misses, the next bomb scored a direct hit followed by another amidships which created a large explosion. The after part of the ship disintegrated and the ship sank in 30–40 seconds. (www.hmshollyhock.com)

According to the British, *Hollyhock* was attacked by two pairs of aircraft. The first pair gained a near miss that put a boiler out of action at 1208hrs and the second pair gained two hits at 1217hrs which sank the corvette in under a minute. From the crew of 65, 75 per cent were killed and 17 per cent wounded.

The last ship to come under attack was the 2,924-ton Norwegian freighter *Norviken*. It was attacked near the location of *Hermes'* demise and hit twice with a third damaging near miss, according to the Norwegians. The Japanese claimed that the six Vals that selected it scored five hits. Whatever the case, the damage killed four crewmen, including the captain. The crew abandoned ship and the *Norviken* drifted ashore the next morning.

Compared to the attack on Trincomalee with 91 Kates, the 85 Vals rendered a much greater return for the Japanese war effort. Dropping 85 bombs, the dive-bombers destroyed six ships, including three warships. The prowess of the dive-bombers prevented the Trincomalee operation from being a crushing disappointment. The Japanese detailed the attacks in the following manner.

Japanese Dive-bombing Results on 9 April 1942

Target	Carrier and Number of Aircraft	Bombs Dropped	Hits	Accuracy Percentage
Hermes	*Akagi* – 2	2	2	100
Hermes	*Hiryu* – 11	11	9	82
Hermes	*Zuikaku* – 14	14	13	93
Hermes	*Shokaku* – 18	18	13	72
Vampire	*Akagi* – 12	12	12	100
Vampire	*Hiryu* – 4	4	1	25
Hollyhock	*Soryu* – 6	6	1	17
British Sergeant	*Akagi* – 3	3	3	100
Athelstane	*Soryu* – 6	6	5	83
British Sergeant	*Hiryu* – 3	3	3	100
Norviken	*Soryu* – 6	6	5	83

Not a single dive-bomber was lost to anti-aircraft fire during this series of attacks. Throughout the battle, the British had severe problems coordinating air cover for naval units by fighters based ashore. As a result, the two cruisers on 5 April were left undefended, as was *Hermes* on 9 April. At least on 9 April the FAA and RAF made a belated appearance when eight Fulmars from 803 and 806 Squadrons at Ratmalana Airfield arrived just after noon as *Athelstane* was sinking. By the time they intervened, the Zeros escorting the Japanese strike had departed since there was no sign of British air opposition. The first group of Fulmars was joined by six more from 273 Squadron from RAF Kokkilai, 35nm north-west of China Bay. The absence of the Zeros set up a fair fight between the cumbersome but well-armed Fulmars and the highly manoeuvrable but under armed dive-bombers. Over the next 25 minutes, four dive-bombers and two Fulmars were downed. Four more dive-bombers were damaged. The delay in finding *Hermes* had exposed the Japanese to danger, as well as Egusa's decision to keep his squadron behind and look for additional targets.

Another victim of *Soryu*'s dive-bombers was the tanker *Athelstane*. The ship's crew stated that in the course of five minutes it was struck by five direct hits and two near misses. Despite this beating, no crewmen were lost. (www.hmshollyhock.com)

Another action on 9 April was the virtually unknown occasion when the Striking Force came under attack for the first time in the war. After the morning Catalina detection of the Striking Force, 11 Blenheims from 11 Squadron launched from the Racecourse at 0820hrs. Two turned back due to engine trouble. As the Japanese dive-bombers were pummelling *Hermes*, the Striking Force had its first experience with an air attack. Nine Blenheims attacked, dropping bombs near *Akagi* and *Tone*. The British counter-attack caught the Japanese completely by surprise. There was no warning, and the first time the Japanese were even aware of the presence of the British bombers was when bomb splashes shot up around *Akagi*. *Akagi* did not even open fire from its anti-aircraft guns. The attack came from about 11,000ft, and thus there was little chance the inexperienced aircrews could hit a ship from that altitude.

Belatedly, the CAP went after the Blenheims and shot down four of them. There were no survivors from any of these aircraft. The 20 Zeros on CAP – six from *Soryu*, eight from *Hiryu* and three each from *Akagi* and *Zuikaku* – claimed 18 Blenheims. One Zero from *Hiryu* was lost in this action. The remaining five aircraft encountered the Japanese aircraft returning from the *Hermes* attack. Between 1135hrs and 1147hrs, the Japanese claimed two of the four bombers. Only one was shot down, along with another Zero from *Hiryu*. The four remaining Blenheims were all damaged but returned to base.

Following the attack on Trincomalee, the Striking Force moved to the east and refuelled on 10 April. According to plan, the force left the Indian Ocean by the Strait of Malacca on 13 April. The next day, the Striking Force split up in the South China Sea. The 5th Carrier Division headed for Truk Atoll in the Central Pacific to prepare for the Port Moresby operation. This unit was selected in part because it was the least well-trained carrier division in the Striking Force and it was thought it could benefit from more seasoning. The other three carriers headed back to Japan to prepare for the Combined Fleet's biggest operation of the war to date – the invasion of Midway Atoll and the expected decisive clash with the USN's Pacific Fleet.

OPERATIONS OF THE MALAYA UNIT STRIKING FORCE

The operations of Ozawa's Malaya Unit Striking Force lasted from 1–11 April. At 1400hrs on 1 April, the bulk of the Malaya Unit departed Mergui in southern Burma. When Ozawa learned on 3 April that *I-7* reported it was unable to make a covert reconnaissance of Colombo, he assumed that this would force Nagumo to move his attack back by one day. Accordingly,

Jim Laurier

STRIKING FORCE UNDER ATTACK (PP. 74–75)

One of the unknown episodes of the Indian Ocean Raid was the first Allied attack on the Striking Force during the entire war. On 9 April, in response to information from a Catalina flying boat earlier in the morning, the British launched their entire striking force available on Ceylon – 11 Blenheim IV bombers from 11 Squadron. The aircraft took off at about 0820hrs from the Racecourse; two were forced to turn back because of engine trouble. After a brief search they found the Striking Force.

The squadron leader decided to target *Akagi* since it was the largest carrier present. The approach of the Blenheims caught the Japanese totally by surprise, with the weakness of the Striking Force's air defence doctrine on full display. None of the Japanese ships carried radar and the Zero fighters on CAP failed to spot the British aircraft.

In this battlescene, the Blenheims (**1**) are conducting their attack from about 10,000ft, dropping a total of 27 500lb and 250lb semi-armour piercing bombs. The aircrew from 11 Squadron had no experience or training in attacking maritime targets so there was little chance they would hit a target, even a surprised one, from this altitude. Three bombs landed near *Akagi*'s bow (**2**), but the other bombs aimed at the carrier and the escorting cruiser *Tone* (**3**) were far off the mark. The totally surprised Japanese did not even open fire with their anti-aircraft guns.

After dropping their bombs, the Blenheims formed a tight formation to make good their escape. The 20 Zeros on CAP responded and shot down four of the retreating bombers. There were no survivors from any of the aircraft. During this melee, one of *Hiryu*'s most experienced Zero pilots was killed. With the British formation shattered and in retreat, the Zeros broke off pursuit in case other British aircraft attempted to attack the carriers. The next time the Striking Force was exposed to air attack during the battle of Midway, it would not be so lucky.

Track of the Malaya Unit, 1–8 April 1942

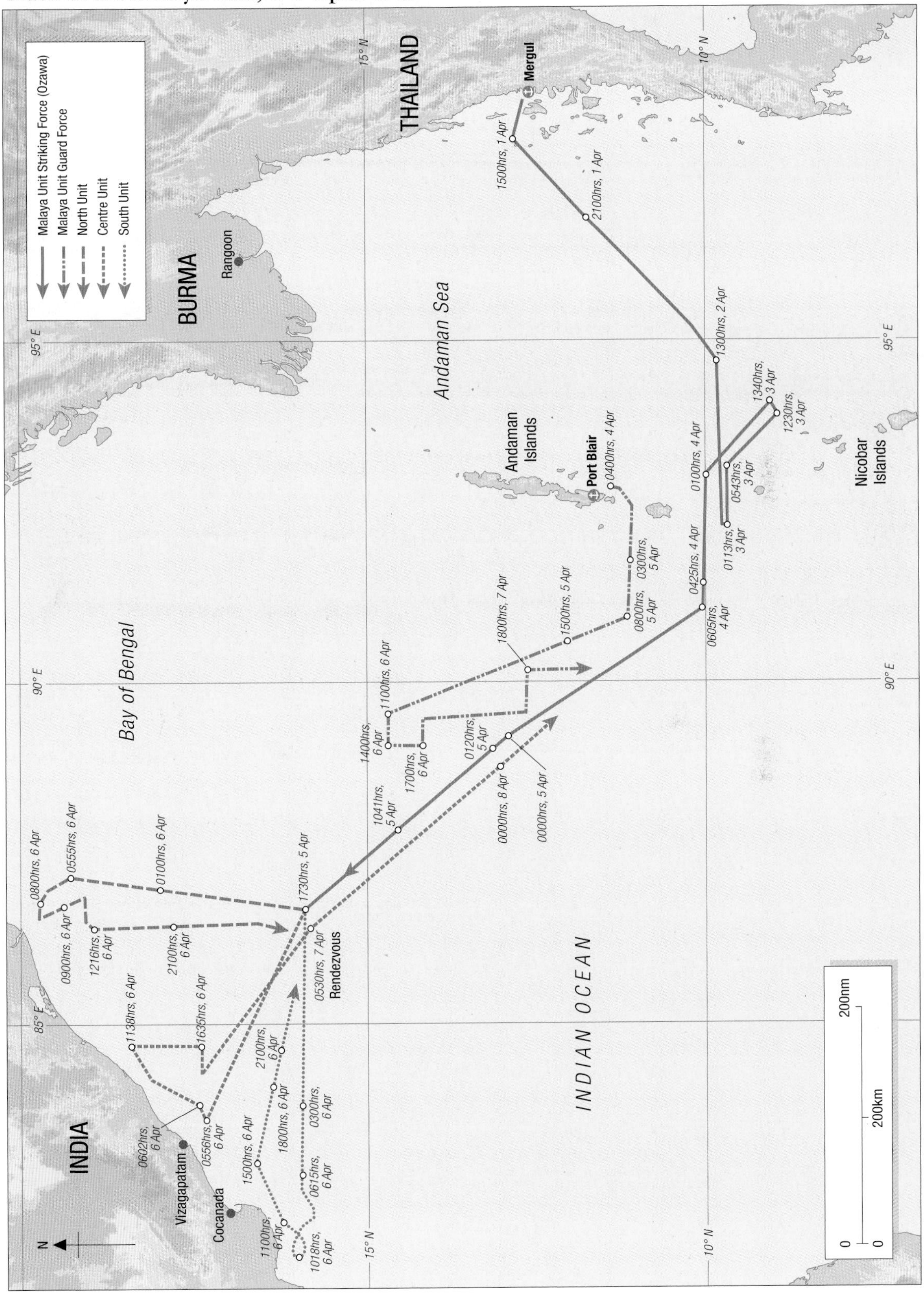

Legend:
- Malaya Unit Striking Force (Ozawa)
- Malaya Unit Guard Force
- North Unit
- Centre Unit
- South Unit

THAILAND

BURMA

Rangoon

Andaman Sea

Mergui

1500hrs, 1 Apr
2100hrs, 1 Apr
1300hrs, 2 Apr
1340hrs, 3 Apr
1230hrs, 3 Apr
0100hrs, 4 Apr
0543hrs, 3 Apr
0113hrs, 3 Apr

Andaman Islands

Port Blair
0400hrs, 4 Apr

Bay of Bengal

0300hrs, 5 Apr
0800hrs, 5 Apr
0425hrs, 4 Apr
0605hrs, 4 Apr
1500hrs, 5 Apr
1800hrs, 7 Apr

1100hrs, 6 Apr
1400hrs, 6 Apr
1700hrs, 6 Apr
0120hrs, 5 Apr
0000hrs, 8 Apr
0000hrs, 5 Apr

1041hrs, 5 Apr

17:30hrs, 5 Apr

0800hrs, 6 Apr
0555hrs, 6 Apr
0100hrs, 6 Apr
0900hrs, 6 Apr
1216hrs, 6 Apr
2100hrs, 6 Apr
1138hrs, 6 Apr
0635hrs, 6 Apr
0530hrs, 7 Apr
Rendezvous

INDIA

Vizagapatam
Cocanada

0602hrs, 6 Apr
0556hrs, 6 Apr
1500hrs, 6 Apr
1800hrs, 6 Apr
0300hrs, 6 Apr
2100hrs, 6 Apr
0615hrs, 6 Apr
1100hrs, 6 Apr
1018hrs, 6 Apr

Nicobar Islands

INDIAN OCEAN

N

200nm
200km

95° E
90° E
85° E
95° E
90° E
15° N
10° N
15° N
10° N

Chokai is shown here in a photo dating from October 1942. During Operation C, it was the flagship of the Malaya Unit Striking Force. (Yamato Museum)

Ozawa ordered the Malaya Unit to also move its attack back by one day. This meant that it reversed course to an area east of the Nicobar Islands and that *Ryujo* suspended search missions until the following day.

On 4 April, the Malaya Unit changed course to the west and headed for Ten Degree Channel. After passing through the channel, the force headed to the north-west towards the point where it would split into three parts. That evening, light cruiser *Sendai*, the 11th Destroyer Division, and the 1st Section of the 19th Destroyer Division headed to a position north-west of Port Blair to guard the rear of the Malaya Unit.

As part of the preparations to deal with the expected Japanese attack, the British had begun to disperse shipping on the east coast of India. The concentration at Calcutta was reduced. There were no escorts available, so the only measure taken was to move the ships south in small convoys as close to the shore as possible. Ozawa was bound to encounter rich pickings.

Ozawa's force was still headed to the north-west when he learned early on 5 April that the air attack on Columbo had occurred. Given this knowledge that the Striking Force had conducted its raid on time, Ozawa ordered the commencement of offensive operations. Between 1133hrs and 1210hrs, *Ryujo* launched ten Kates carrying six 132lb bombs each to search the area 260–280nm to the north-west. Between 1340hrs and 1442hrs, the aircraft spotted ten merchant ships, two of which were bombed. Six of these aircraft found targets. The 5,082-ton *Harpasa* was sunk with six killed; *Dardanus*, a 7,823-ton freighter, was disabled but was taken under tow; *Point Clear* (4,839 tons) was damaged.

The locations of *Ryujo*'s contacts indicated that the shipping lanes were within 30nm of the Indian coast. Ozawa changed the operating areas of

his three subunits to reflect this information. At 1730hrs, the Malaya Unit reached the point where the force divided into three sections.

The Malaya Unit Striking Force began its operations against Allied shipping on 6 April. Results were immediate against the undefended shipping that teemed in the area. The Centre Unit (*Ryujo*, heavy cruiser *Chokai*, light cruiser *Yura* and destroyer *Yugiri*) reached its designated operations area at about 0600hrs. *Ryujo* launched four Kates and *Chokai* launched its floatplanes.

Ryujo's aircraft damaged the 5,491-ton American freighter *Bienville*. The damaged merchant was overtaken by *Chokai* and *Ryujo* and finished off by gunfire and a single torpedo. Nineteen crewmembers were killed. A single floatplane from *Chokai* scored a near miss on the 6,245-ton British freighter *Ganges*. Minutes later, the British crew spotted a destroyer and two more aircraft from *Ryujo*. After one of the aircraft set the deck cargo on fire with a direct hit, the destroyer was joined by *Chokai*, *Yura* and *Ryujo* which all proceeded to pound the defenceless ship until it sank with the loss of 11 crewmen. The final victim in this area was the 2,646-ton British merchant *Sinkiang*. It was first attacked by a single aircraft and then finished off by *Chokai*.

Ozawa detached *Yura* and *Yugiri* to operate closer to the coast in search of additional victims. They encountered and sank two small Dutch merchants (*Banjoewangi*, 1,279 tons with 13 killed, and the 1,279-ton *Batavia* with four crewmen lost), and the 3,471-ton British merchant *Taksang* with 15 dead.

The final two ships dispatched by the Centre Unit were sunk by aircraft. The 5,686-ton American *Selma City* was first attacked by a floatplane from *Chokai*. The Japanese crew scored a direct hit which caused a fire

This is destroyer *Yugiri* pictured in 1930 conducting sea trials. Its appearance was little changed by 1942. *Yugiri* was one of the destroyers assigned to the Malaya Unit and contributed to the sinking of three merchant ships during Operation C. (Yamato Museum)

Ryujo shown in 1938. It took two major modifications to rectify its original flawed design. Despite lingering limitations, it performed well in the Dutch East Indies campaign and during the Indian Ocean raid against weak Allied resistance. (Yamato Museum)

and prompted the captain to order the crew to abandon ship. As this was occurring, two *Ryujo* bombers appeared and scored two more hits. The ship later sank, but the entire crew survived. The small Dutch merchant *Van der Capellen* (2,073 tons) was attacked by two *Ryujo* bombers. The ship was damaged and succumbed on 8 April. The last ship attacked by *Ryujo*'s busy air group was the 5,268-ton British freighter *Anglo-Canadian*. Despite being attacked by five Kates, two armed with torpedoes, it dodged all but a single bomb (which did not explode) and survived.

In addition to their attacks on maritime targets, *Ryujo*'s small air group launched three attacks, each with five bombers, on Vizagapatam and Cocanada in mainland India. The attacks were launched at 1143hrs, 1330hrs and 1655hrs, with two directed at Vizagapatam. Nine merchants and four small warships were present in the harbour, but only one merchant was hit by a bomb that failed to explode. The single raid on Cocanada failed to hit either of the two merchants present. According to Japanese sources, the aircraft were tasked with hitting targets ashore; in neither location was any significant damage recorded.

The Southern Unit (heavy cruisers *Mikuma* and *Mogami*, and destroyer *Amagiri*) also enjoyed success. When they reached their designated objective area, the cruisers launched scout aircraft. These reported two transports at 0730hrs. By the afternoon, the force had sunk four ships: *Gandara* towing the disabled *Dardanus*; and two Norwegian ships, *Dagfred* (4,434 tons) and *Hermod* (1,515 tons). Only 15 men from *Gandara* were lost. To do this, the cruisers used 257 8in rounds and *Amagiri* 78 5in shells and three torpedoes. Nine bombs were dropped from the floatplanes.

The North Unit (heavy cruisers *Kumano* and *Suzuya*, and destroyer *Shirakumo*) under Rear Admiral Kurita Takeo had even more luck. The floatplanes from the cruisers were launched at about 0600hrs and within 45 minutes had spotted seven ships. Using 523 8in and 250 5in rounds from the cruisers, and 200 5in rounds from the destroyer, all seven ships were sunk. The targets were engaged from an average range of 5,500–6,500 yards, and it took on average 75 8in shells to sink one merchant ship. As the skipper of *Mogami* observed, it proved difficult to sink merchant ships with 8in armour-piercing shells. The seven ships dispatched in only three hours included: *Elsa*, a Norwegian tanker of 5,381 tons (one killed); British freighter *Malda*, 9,066 tons with 25 dead; *Autolycus*, another British freighter of 7,718 tons with at least 11 dead; British freighter *Indora*, 6,622 tons with two dead; American freighter *Exmoor*, 4,986 tons; British freighter *Silksworth*, 4,921 tons; and the small British freighter *Shinkuang*, 2,441 tons with three dead.

The floatplanes were used to strafe the bridges of the ships from the west, thus preventing their retreat close to shore. When returning to the cruisers, the two floatplanes were engaged by three 'Hurricanes' (actually Curtiss P-36 Mohawks from 5 Squadron RAF). The Dave floatplane from *Kumano* was shot up, but no crewmen were wounded or killed. After recovering the floatplanes, the cruisers spotted a large merchant afire to the west. The ship was dispatched, and having no more contacts, the Northern Force set course to the south to rejoin the rest of the Malaya Unit.

The Nakajima E8N Type 95 'Dave' was the predominant floatplane on the escorts of the Striking Force in April 1942. This is a Dave on light cruiser *Nagara* at Shanghai in 1936. Because of its short range and slow cruising speed, the Dave was unsuited to the role of reconnaissance aircraft. (Naval History and Heritage Command)

Kumano pictured in March 1939 after its conversion into a heavy cruiser. All four of the powerful Mogami-class heavy cruisers were committed to Operation C and were assigned to the Malaya Unit Striking Force. (Yamato Museum)

By 0530hrs on 7 April, the Malaya Unit had reunited and was steaming south-east towards the Nicobar Islands. Ozawa's fleet reached the Strait of Malacca on the evening of 9 April and anchored in Singapore on the morning of 11 April. From there, almost all the ships were sent to Japan in preparation for Stage Two operations. After the claims from the three subunits were tallied, the Malaya Unit claimed the destruction of 21 merchantmen of approximately 137,000 tons and damage to eight more of some 47,000 tons. The only damage suffered by Ozawa's force was the 19 bullet holes incurred by the floatplane from *Kumano*. In reality, the Japanese sank 20 ships of 93,247 tons and damaged three more of 13,934 tons. Official British sources give the incorrect total of 23 ships sunk by Ozawa's force.

JAPANESE SUBMARINE OPERATIONS

Operation C was supported by the 2nd Submarine Squadron. Of the seven large submarines assigned to this unit, only five were ready at the start of the operation. *I-1* was forced to return to Japan because of engine trouble, and *I-5* ran aground in the entrance to Kendari on 28 February and efforts were still being made to refloat it as the other five boats departed. *I-5* joined the operation late, departing Kendari on 25 March. During a brief patrol off Ceylon, it reported making no attacks.

The commander of Submarine Unit C was Rear Admiral Ichioka on *I-7*. *I-7* had an important role to play in the operation since it was assigned to

Japanese Submarine Operations during Operation C

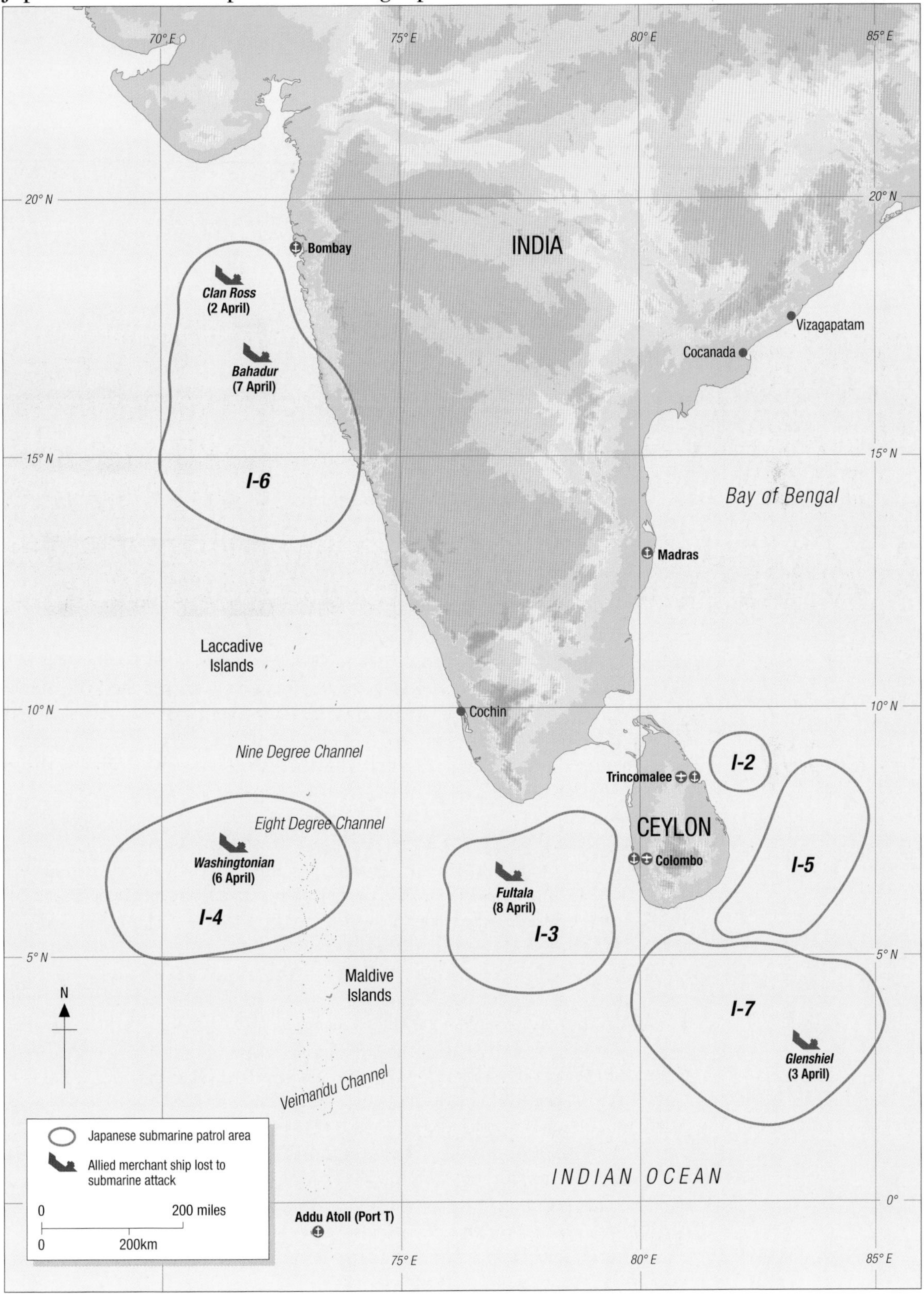

70° E
75° E
80° E
85° E
20° N
15° N
10° N
5° N
0°
INDIA
Bombay
Clan Ross
(2 April)
Bahadur
(7 April)
I-6
Vizagapatam
Cocanada
Bay of Bengal
Madras
Laccadive
Islands
Cochin
Nine Degree Channel
Trincomalee
I-2
Eight Degree Channel
CEYLON
Washingtonian
(6 April)
Colombo
I-5
Fultala
(8 April)
I-4
I-3
Maldive
Islands
I-7
N
Glenshiel
(3 April)
Veimandu Channel
Japanese submarine patrol area
Allied merchant ship lost to
submarine attack
INDIAN OCEAN
0
200 miles
0
200km
Addu Atoll (Port T)

The crew of Type J3 submarine *I-7* is lined up abaft the sail hiding the presence of the catapult to launch the small E14Y1 'Glen' floatplane. Part of IJN doctrine was to use these large aircraft-carrying submarines to reconnoitre defended bases to locate enemy fleet units. This was *I-7*'s mission in Operation C which it failed to perform. (Yamato Museum)

conduct a reconnaissance of Colombo and Trincomalee two days before the scheduled air attack. From the start, *I-7* had difficulty in carrying out the mission. On 1 April, it was attacked by a flying boat 180nm south-east of Ceylon after dark. British patrol activity forced a cancellation of the floatplane reconnaissance late on the 2nd. Early on 3 April, the submarine encountered the British merchant *Glenshiel* and sank it with two torpedoes and 20 shells from its deck gun.

I-3 had the commander of the 7th Submarine Division onboard. It departed Penang on 28 March and headed to Colombo where it was ordered to scout enemy movements and provide weather updates. It also found it difficult to penetrate the waters near Colombo as indicated in a report sent on 3 April. On 5 April, it had moved to within 36nm of the port and sent two weather reports. By the morning of 7 April it was 100–150nm west of Colombo and spotted seven merchants in the morning. *I-3* attacked three of them with a total or four torpedoes and 39 shells, but only claimed shell damage to one, the *British Elmdale*. The next day, it encountered a merchant about 180nm west of Colombo and attacked it with one torpedo. This marked the end of British merchant *Fultala* (5,051 tons).

I-2 also departed Penang on 28 March, but headed for Trincomalee. On 3 April, it arrived at the objective and sent a report on the state of enemy activity and the weather near Trincomalee. During the Japanese air attacks on 9 April, *I-2* witnessed the destruction of several British ships. It departed the next day for Singapore after making no attacks on an Allied target.

I-4 departed Penang and was sent to watch the Eight Degree Channel. On 6 April it attacked the American *Washingtonian* (6,617 tons) in the western part of the channel and dispatched it with two torpedoes.

I-6 departed Penang on 26 March and was assigned to attack traffic off Bombay. On 31 March, it claimed a mid-sized cargo ship to the east of the Eight Degree Channel. Two days later, it encountered and sank the British ship *Clan Ross* (5,897 tons) off Bombay with three torpedoes. *I-6* remained off Bombay and sank another ship, the *British Bahadur* (5,424 tons) on 7 April after expending seven torpedoes and eight shells.

Following the air attack on Trincomalee on 9 April, Ichioka ordered his boats to leave their stations and return to Singapore. The submarines arrived there between 15 and 17 April without loss. The Japanese tally for the six submarines participating in Operation C was six merchants (five confirmed) and four motorized sailing ships. Allied records confirm that this short offensive accounted for five merchant ships of 32,404 tons. This was a disappointing result given the density of Allied shipping in the area. More importantly, the submarines had provided no intelligence to the Striking Force regarding the locations and operations of Allied naval units. This was one of the last occasions during the war that Japanese submarines were ordered to use their short-range floatplanes to conduct reconnaissance of a defended port. The Japanese later recognized that this tactic was no longer tenable. They also criticized the deployment of the few submarines available for Operation C, stating that they were too spread out and would have been better used had they all been concentrated near Colombo.

This is J1 Type submarine *I-3* photographed in 1930. These *junsen* (cruiser) submarines were designed for long-range raiding or reconnaissance operations. They were heavily armed with 20 torpedoes and two 5.5in deck guns. Though used in their intended role during Operation C, they were only minimally successful. (Yamato Museum)

OPERATION C – THE FINAL ACCOUNTING

By the time the Striking Force headed east on 9 April, it was apparent that the Imperial Navy had scored another impressive victory. In total, seven Allied warships had been sunk. These ranged from the dated and almost useless carrier *Hermes* to an armed merchant cruiser about to be decommissioned, two old destroyers of little value, a corvette and two heavy cruisers. By far the most valuable ships were the two heavy cruisers, and this loss constituted 50 per cent of RN heavy cruiser losses during the entire war.

Allied merchant losses were heavy but far from crippling. Between the efforts of the Malaya Unit Striking Force, the submarines and Nagumo's aviators, 29 Allied merchant ships were lost. Allied air losses were also heavy but by no means crippling. Forty-seven aircraft were lost in the air and another 17 on the ground or on merchant *Sagaing* sunk in Trincomalee harbour.

Indian Ocean Losses, 2–9 April 1942

Category	British	Japanese
Warships	7	0
Merchant ships	29	0
Aircraft	54	18
Men	1,028	32

The only Japanese losses were to the aircraft and aviators of the Striking Force. In total, 18 aircraft were lost – six Zeros, 10 Vals and two Kates. Thirty-one additional aircraft were damaged. Since the Striking Force began Operation C with 275 aircraft, this constituted a loss rate of 7 per cent. While not negligible, it in no way hampered subsequent operations.

AFTERMATH

The results of the IJN's Indian Ocean raid were indecisive. Nagumo's primary mission was the destruction of the Eastern Fleet. The Japanese failed to gain this objective. They inflicted significant attrition on the Eastern Fleet, but despite having the opportunity to do so, failed to destroy it. However, the Eastern Fleet was forced to forfeit control of the eastern Indian Ocean. British air power on Ceylon was temporarily shattered with over a third of the fighter force and most of the small strike force destroyed in only two days of combat. Had the Japanese desired, they could have certainly secured Ceylon by invasion. Furthermore, shipping along the eastern coast of India was paralysed. The huge port of Calcutta was shut down and by the end of April traffic remained at a standstill. Traffic at lesser ports on the eastern coast also came to a virtual stop.

All of these effects were unimportant since the Japanese were unable to follow up their raid with concerted operations to establish sea control of key areas. This made any success achieved in April 1942 fleeting. Japanese strategic success in the Indian Ocean proved to be a chimera.

Even though the Japanese failed to destroy the Eastern Fleet, the result easily could have been different. In fact, the only thing that saved Somerville's fleet from disaster and perhaps virtual destruction was Japanese incompetence.

Shiranui pictured during the Indian Ocean raid taking on fuel from battleship *Kongo*. The Kagero class was the most modern class of Japanese destroyers at the start of the war, so they were assigned to the Striking Force. (Yamato Museum)

This is a Zero taking off from *Zuikaku* on 20 January 1942 during the attack on Rabaul. The Zero was the best carrier fighter of the period and outclassed all but a few British fighters during the April 1942 Indian Ocean raid. (Yamato Museum)

The shortcomings of Nagumo and his staff were significant. These stemmed from an overall lack of flexibility and imagination. The Striking Force's primary mission was the destruction of the Eastern Fleet. To accomplish this, Nagumo assumed he would catch the British fleet in harbour. His assumption that he would achieve surprise was proved incorrect on 4 April when the Striking Force was detected on its approach to Colombo. In spite of being detected early and obviously losing the possibility of surprise, Nagumo adhered to the original plan. Not surprisingly, on 5 April Colombo was found to be devoid of major warships. The pathetic Japanese search plan for 5 April indicates that Nagumo still believed he would catch the British by surprise, thus making search operations superfluous. His only concession to the changed situation was to keep a larger reserve of aircraft to deal with unforeseen developments. This proved useful in the hours following the Colombo attack when Japanese search aircraft stumbled upon two heavy cruisers. These were quickly sunk by dive-bombers, representing the most important success in the entire operation.

If the Eastern Fleet was not in harbour, then it had to be at sea. The lack of a robust search plan on 5 April made finding the Eastern Fleet at sea unlikely. Using only five search aircraft, all short-ranged floatplanes, for a morning search with no other searches planned for the remainder of the day was beyond negligent. This is even more inexplicable given the signs the Japanese received about a British carrier force operating in the area. The fact that the two cruisers were headed at high speed to the south-west was a clue, but the interception of the Albacores later in the afternoon so far away from Ceylon was an unmistakable indicator of a nearby British carrier. Nagumo lacked the imagination to understand that his opportunity to achieve his mission was staring him in the face. Instead, he stuck to his original plan and manoeuvred away from where the Eastern Fleet was located. The serious search made on 6 April inevitably turned up nothing.

Nagumo's lack of flexibility and imagination could have been overcome by the simple precaution of mounting a serious air search in the waters around the Striking Force. The doctrine of using only floatplanes from the

The Eastern Fleet possessed an imposing total of five battleships. However, four of these were dated and not modernized Royal Sovereign-class units. This is *Resolution* pictured leading *Formidable*. Despite this photograph, *Resolution* and its sister ships were too slow to operate with the much faster fleet carriers. (Royal Navy, now in the Public Domain)

escorting cruisers and battleships was dangerous since the number of aircraft was inadequate for a full search and almost all of the aircraft were short ranged. On 5 April, the Eastern Fleet operated within Japanese search range for most of the day and was never spotted. Nevertheless, Nagumo thought it more important to use six of his carrier attack bombers as guide aircraft for the returning Colombo strike than to use them to augment his search effort. The use of just these six aircraft for search missions would have likely resulted in the discovery of the Eastern Fleet and a much different outcome for the entire battle.

Another indication of Nagumo's inflexibility was his decision to stick with the original plan and attack Trincomalee. It was illogical to think that since the Eastern Fleet was not in Colombo then it could be in Trincomalee just four days later. Of course, there was no chance the British fleet would have returned to port in only a matter of days with a massive Japanese carrier force loose in the area.

In the attacks on both Colombo and Trincomalee the target selection did not coincide with Nagumo's main objective. Nagumo knew he was conducting a raid and not preparing Ceylon for invasion. Therefore, any effort by relatively few bombers to destroy the naval bases and airfields was wasted since such small attacks could produce only temporary effects. All the bombers should have been allocated to attack the shipping which was present in both harbours.

From the Japanese perspective, the only thing that kept Operation C from being a gigantic waste of time and effort was the premature dispersion of the Eastern Fleet that exposed parts of it to destruction. Looking at Operation C with perfect hindsight, Yamamoto should not have bothered to endorse an Indian Ocean adventure at all. The time gained could have been used to prepare the Striking Force for Phase Two operations. These were much more important than dealing with the non-existent threat from the Eastern Fleet.

Late on the morning of 9 April 1942, *Hermes* began its final plunge off Ceylon's eastern coast. In this view, the carrier is on fire. Smoke can be seen issuing from some of the holes caused by bomb hits. Casualties were high with 306 crewmen killed. (Imperial Japanese Navy, now in the Public Domain)

Had Yamamoto considered Phase Two operations more carefully, he could have used the extra time to employ the entire Striking Force in the South Pacific to conduct the Port Moresby operation (Operation *MO*) followed by his grand operation against Midway Atoll (Operation *MI*).

As bad as Nagumo's performance was, Somerville's was perhaps worse. As commander of the much weaker force, he had little room for error. In spite of his clear orders to preserve the Eastern Fleet and avoid the massive damage to British fortunes should his fleet be destroyed, Somerville committed a series of blunders that exposed his force to potential destruction. Somerville's poor use of intelligence and his creation of a poorly thought out set of assumptions led directly to his flawed positioning between 31 March and 2 April. Had the Japanese begun their raid during these dates, it is almost certain that disaster would have befallen the Eastern Fleet. Another potential disaster could have resulted from Somerville's decision to rush from Port T to the east after he learned of the Japanese attack on Colombo on 5 April. This was a reckless move without knowing the strength of the Japanese force, but enough information existed in the immediate aftermath of the Japanese air raid on Colombo for Somerville to correctly surmise that his previous assessments on the strength of the Japanese carrier force were greatly in error. Somerville's plan of staying beyond the range of Japanese air searches during the day and then closing the distance at night almost came to fruition on 5 April. This was also a high-risk tactic and was only given a chance to succeed because of Nagumo's incompetence.

Somerville was known as a fighting admiral. In April 1942, this reputation may have been part of the reason he risked his fleet against a superior opponent. In so doing, he directly disobeyed the orders of the Admiralty and chiefs of staff to exercise a fleet in being concept. Willis and Layton both had issues with Somerville's actions. Willis later described Somerville's actions as possibly driven by a desire not to repeat a November 1940 incident when the Admiralty accused him of being insufficiently aggressive in his pursuit of an Italian naval force. The Eastern Fleet survived April 1942 due to sheer luck in spite of Somerville's determination to expose it to the maximum amount of risk possible without verging into recklessness.

The most tangible Japanese successes during Operation C were the sinking of the two cruisers and *Hermes*. These were entirely avoidable disasters. When the Japanese raid on Ceylon failed to unfold as predicted, Somerville made the decision to disperse the Eastern Fleet too quickly. Until the situation was clarified, sending the two cruisers to Colombo was wrong. Sending *Hermes* to Trincomalee was the precursor to another minor disaster.

Arbuthnot also made questionable decisions. He should have ordered *Hermes* to leave Trincomalee immediately upon the discovery of the Striking Force on 8 April. Had *Hermes* and the other ships in harbour left as soon as possible, instead of 'as convenient' as Arbuthnot's orders allowed, and had they headed as far south as possible, instead of only 40nm away, they almost certainly would not have been spotted by Japanese search aircraft on the morning of 9 April. Arbuthnot's explanation immediately after the battle that the loss of *Hermes* was due to bad luck, and not any error on his part, is disingenuous at best.

In the aftermath of the April raid, the British expected further Japanese raids into the Indian Ocean and a continuing threat for the invasion of Ceylon. To prevent a calamity in the form of the Japanese cutting oil shipments from the Persian Gulf, the British decided that preserving the Eastern Fleet was more important than holding Ceylon. Therefore, the fleet was withdrawn to East Africa. It would have to be built up before it could return to the central Indian Ocean. Defence of Ceylon would have to depend on air power alone.

Somerville remained in command of the Eastern Fleet after the events of April 1942. After his near-death experience with the Striking Force, Somerville became a convert to the power of Japanese naval aviation. As a result, he handled his fleet very conservatively for the rest of 1942. Following the Japanese raid, the bulk of the Eastern Fleet moved to the safety of Kilindini in Kenya and waited for reinforcement. Kilindini remained the Eastern Fleet's primary base for the rest of 1942, but as the fleet grew stronger, Somerville began to operate around Ceylon on a regular basis. In May, carrier *Illustrious* joined the fleet. In July, the core of the fleet was two modern carriers, modernized battleships *Warspite* and *Valiant*, the almost worthless *Royal Sovereign* and *Resolution*, one heavy cruiser, three modern 6in cruisers, six older cruisers and nine modern destroyers. Somerville also had the time to conduct training and turn the Eastern Fleet into a cohesive force. With the reinforced Eastern Fleet and additional aircraft on Ceylon, the British assessed they could hold Ceylon in the increasingly unlikely event the Japanese attempted a full invasion. The Pedestal convoy in August and the invasion of North Africa in November reduced the Eastern Fleet's strength but following the Japanese defeat at Midway in June and the full-scale battle of attrition at Guadalcanal between the IJN and the USN that began in August and ran through the end of the year, the threat of a major Japanese move into the Indian Ocean had all but disappeared. The period of the United Kingdom's great vulnerability in the Indian Ocean had passed.

After the raid the IJN prepared for Phase Two operations. After its high-water mark in the Indian Ocean, the Striking Force was broken up. The 5th Carrier Division was allocated to support operations in the South Pacific with the objective of seizing Port Moresby on New Guinea. With two USN carriers in the region, the result was the first carrier battle of the war in the Coral Sea. Rear Admiral Hara commanded the Striking Force covering the invasion and his performance was better than Nagumo's the previous month. Nevertheless, *Shokaku* was heavily damaged by American dive-bombers and *Zuikaku*'s air group took such heavy losses it was unavailable for Yamamoto's main operation in early June aimed at Midway Atoll.

At Midway, the full array of issues that the Striking Force exhibited off Ceylon were replayed with greater effect. In so many ways, Operation C was a dress rehearsal for Midway. The Japanese saw some of their weaknesses during Operation C and took measures to address them. These sticking plasters could not alleviate the systemic and doctrinal weaknesses of the Striking Force. The result was the destruction of *Akagi*, *Kaga*, *Soryu* and *Hiryu* off Midway.

Comparing Operation C and Operation *MI* in detail provides insight into the reasons behind the Japanese debacle at Midway. In planning both operations, the Japanese assumed they would gain strategic and tactical surprise. However, in both cases, the Allies had broken the IJN's operational codes and had advance warning of the operations. In both cases, this insight was imperfect. For Operation C, the British were aware of the original attack date instead of the actual one four days later. To fill in the gaps of the Japanese plan, the British made a series of assumptions almost all of which were wrong. For the Midway operation, the Americans were also off on the original attack date versus the actual attack date, but in this case the difference was only one day. The Americans were also forced to make a series of assumptions for planning purposes, but in their case they were mostly correct. For both operations, the likelihood that the Japanese could gain tactical surprise was much reduced by the fact that Allied flying boats were searching 500–600nm from the respective Japanese objectives.

In both operations, Japanese submarines failed in their mission to provide warning for the Striking Force. In April, the submarines failed to detect Eastern Fleet units near the naval bases at Colombo or Trincomalee and failed to discover the presence of the secret base at Addu Atoll. The planned reconnaissance of Colombo by a submarine floatplane was cancelled because of heavy British patrols. Not having learned from these failures, Yamamoto gave the submarines similar responsibilities for Operation *MI*. Again, Japanese submarines failed to detect the movement of American carrier forces from their base at Pearl Harbor to their ambush positions off Midway. A planned reconnaissance of Pearl Harbor by large flying boats using submarines to refuel them at a supposedly desolate location was cancelled because of the presence of American patrols.

One of most salient failures of the Striking Force in both April and June was in reconnaissance. The Japanese underlined the importance of reconnaissance in general after Operation C, but this did not stop them from making the same mistakes at Midway. On both occasions, the Striking Force's search plan was poorly planned and inadequately resourced. Only five search aircraft were used on the morning of 5 April and only seven on the morning of 4 June. These numbers were obviously inadequate for a full search, but on both occasions the Japanese were bedevilled by bad luck. On 5 April, British ships were spotted by a floatplane four hours after it was launched as the aircraft was on its return leg; on 4 June, the same thing occurred but after only three hours following its launch. Problems for the Japanese did not stop after the search aircraft made contact. Though the Japanese recognized after Operation C that the weak ship recognition skills of the reconnaissance aircraft crews had to be improved, the same problem resurfaced in the Midway battle. On both occasions the uncertainty regarding enemy ship types led to considerable confusion and delay.

Just as they were during Operation C, the Japanese were surprised by the sudden appearance of an American task force at Midway. Just as during Operation C, Nagumo had a reserve force in place to deal with such an eventuality. But in a parallel development to events on 5 April, on 4 June the Japanese had already begun to rearm their reserve aircraft with weapons to strike land targets. Again, Nagumo was forced to make a quick armament change on his reserve aircraft. Just as in April, this took longer than expected. At Midway, Nagumo opted for a massive strike by both dive-bombers and torpedo-bombers, whereas on 5 April he launched the dive-bombers two hours after sighting the British ships. The torpedo-bombers would not have launched until four hours after sighting the British cruisers. In both cases the rearming of the Kates with torpedoes was painfully slow. At Midway, this delay was fatal. Failure to launch the available strike aircraft immediately meant that the Striking Force was attacked about two and a half hours after the American ships were sighted with the result of *Akagi*, *Kaga* and *Soryu* being disabled.

In both Operations C and *MI*, the Striking Force was tasked to deliver knockout blows to installations while remaining on alert for the potential appearance of enemy naval forces. If only one threat emerged at a time, this was not an issue but when Nagumo had to decide in the moment how to deal with two threats, the lack of agility by him and his staff became apparent. On both occasions, the senior Japanese aviator recommended a second attack on the initial objectives, Colombo and Midway. This was almost a foregone event given how hard it was to destroy a large facility with a single strike. This recommendation led to Nagumo's decision to order the rearming of his reserve aircraft with land bombs. After their difficulty with this scenario in April, the Japanese should have been better prepared to deal with a repeat situation in June.

Aside from the Japanese problems with reconnaissance, the Striking Force's other major problem was with air defence. This problem was of no consequence against a few Blenheims untrained for maritime attack, but against American dive-bombers the result was much different. The basic problem was the lack of radar as the Japanese highlighted as early as after Operation C. The lack of radar meant that early warning was problematic; combined with the lack of fighter direction against even known threats the Striking Force was vulnerable to air attack. This weakness was so severe that the concept of massing all the Striking Force's carriers together should have been called into question.

The weakness of the Eastern Fleet and of offensive air power on Ceylon meant the Striking Force did not pay for its operational blunders and doctrinal shortcomings in April. Against a peer force like the USN at Midway, such weaknesses resulted in total disaster. Operation C may not have proved to be a decisive event in itself, but it did foreshadow the destruction of the Striking Force and a dramatic change in the fortunes of war in the Pacific.

FURTHER READING

Banks, Arthur, *Wings of the Dawning*, Malvern Publishing Company, Upton-upon-Severn (1996)

Boyd, Andrew, *The Royal Navy in Eastern Waters*, Seaforth Publishing, Barnsley (2017)

Clancy, John, *The Most Dangerous Moment of the War*, Casemate Publishers, Oxford (2015)

Dull, Paul, *A Battle History of the Imperial Japanese Navy (1941–1945)*, Naval Institute Press, Annapolis, MD (1978)

Japanese Research Division, Military History Section, Headquarters, United States Army Forces, Far East, *Japanese Monograph No. 113 (Navy) Task Force Operations*, Tokyo (n.d.)

Kirby, Woodburn, *The War Against Japan, Volume II*, HMSO, London (1958)

Marder, Arthur J., Jacobsen, Mark and Horsfield, John, *Old Friends New Enemies, Volume II: The Pacific War, 1942–45*, Clarendon Press, Oxford (1990)

Ministry of Defence (Navy), *War With Japan, Volume II*, HMSO, London (1995)

Naval Staff, *Battle Summary No. 15 Naval Operations off Ceylon 29th March to 10th April, 1942*, Admiralty (1943)

Piegzik, Michal A., *The Darkest Hour, Volumes 1 & 2*, Helion, Warwick (2022)

Shores, Christopher, Cull, Brian and Izawa, Yasuho, *Bloody Shambles, Volume Two*, Grub Street, London (1993)

Stephenson, Charles, *The Eastern Fleet and the Indian Ocean 1942–44*, Pen & Sword Maritime, Barnsley (2020)

Tagaya, Osamu, *Aichi Type 99 Kanbaku 'Val' Units 1937–42*, Osprey Publishing, Botley (2011)

Tomlinson, Michael, *The Most Dangerous Moment*, William Kimber, London (1976)

War History Office of the National Defense College of Japan, *The Operations of the Navy in the Dutch East Indies and the Bay of Bengal*, Leiden University Press (2018) (this is a translated version of War History Series Volume 26 published in Japanese in 1969)

Unpublished manuscripts found at www.combinedfleet.com:

Kōichiro Kageyama, National Institute for Defense Studies, War History Department, *The Third Mobile Operation in the Indian Ocean (C Operation)* (n.d.)

Stuart, Robert, *A Detailed Analysis of the Attack on Colombo* (2022)

Stuart, Robert, *A Detailed Analysis of the Loss of Cornwall and Dorsetshire* (2019)

Stuart, Robert, *State of the Art: The Japanese Attacks on Hermes, Vampire, Hollyhock, Athelstane, British Sergeant and Norviken, 9 April 1942* (2018)

Stuart, Robert, *91 Bombs: The Japanese Attack on Trincomalee* (2017)

Stuart, Robert, *20 Ships, Not 23: Ozawa's Score, 5–6 April 1942* (2015)

INDEX

Figures in **bold** refer to illustrations. Some caption locators are in brackets.